REVISED A

MARITIME
TERROR

REVISED AND UPDATED

MARITIME TERROR

Protecting Yourself, Your Vessel, and Your Crew against Piracy

• • • ▬ ▬ ▬ • • •

Jim Gray, Mark Monday,
Gary Stubblefield

Paladin Press • Boulder, Colorado

Maritime Terror:
Protecting Yourself, Your Vessel, and Your Crew against Piracy
by Jim Gray, Mark Monday, and Gary Stubblefield

ISBN 13: 978-1-61004-522-3
Printed in the United States of America

Published by Paladin Press, a division of
Paladin Enterprises, Inc.
Gunbarrel Tech Center
7077 Winchester Circle
Boulder, Colorado 80301 USA
+1.303.443.7250

Direct inquiries and/or orders to the above address.

Visit our website at www.paladin-press.com

CONTENTS

— —

This book is dedicated to all seafarers who risk their lives and fortunes on the waters of the world—today, yesterday, and tomorrow.

We owe special thanks to our mentors on the bridge and at the keyboard:

Capt. Frank Gillies, J. Bowyer Bell, Bob Early, Alex Moser, Emil Sarpa, and Hans Halberstadt. Special thanks are owed our editor, Jon Ford, who guided us through the treacherous waters of publishing like a pilot at the bar.

To them all, we wish fair winds and calm seas.

WARNING

The procedures, drills, and techniques outlined in this book are intended *for academic study only*. It is not the intent of the authors, publisher, or distributors of this book to encourage readers to perform any of the procedures, drills, or techniques described herein without proper professional training and supervision.

PREFACE

The vessel, be it a humble merchant ship or a luxury mega-yacht, travels the oceans of the world. Depending on its schedule and routing, the ship could sail through the Gulf of Aden, the Indian Ocean, and on through the Malacca Strait. It could be at an anchorage waiting for passage up a narrow waterway to a pier in an exotic land. Each of these evolutions produces unique security concerns: everything from the theft of personal and ship's gear, to stowaways, to the hijacking of the vessel and ransom demands, and even the murder of its crew. Such is the maritime world of the 21st century.

For the sailing master and crew, the security of their vessel is 24-hours-a-day, 7-days-a-week concern. The purpose of this book is to make the reader aware of the real danger of piracy and other maritime criminal elements. Travel by water is becoming increasingly problematic.

The recent high-profile hijackings for ransom off Somalia, the increase in piracy in the Asian region, and an explosive stowaway problem in several refugee-ridden regions of the world are all examples of the difficulties all modern seamen—whether ship captains or yacht owners—face. Too often they face these problems alone and unprepared.

Pirates are a worldwide problem, but they are not the only problem. Their cousins in crime, maritime terrorists, are taking aim at ships, too. The hijacking of the *Achille Lauro* in 1985, the waterside ambush campaign against Nile tourist cruisers conducted by the rebel group Gama'a in the 1990s, and the suicide bombing of the USS *Cole* in 2000 are all prominent examples of this evolving threat. Today's terrorists have studied these incidents to improve attack techniques against naval vessels, yachts, and particularly commercial shipping.

As a result of all this criminal maritime activity, insurance rates in troubled areas have risen dramatically. The probable losses in 2010 from all causes related to piracy alone were estimated in the billions.

This manual is designed to help the modern sailor make sure the adventure of yachting or steaming on freighters or tankers in piracy-prone shipping routes doesn't turn into catastrophe. The book is not a magic shield: it will not turn bullets; it will not blast would-be marauders off a gangplank. However, the information here is one piece of a comprehensive program that should include formulating, provisioning, training, and testing of a vessel security plan to ensure that you are as safe as you can be in a world that is itself uncertain and unsafe.

INTRODUCTION:

THE INCREASING THREAT OF MARITIME CRIME

Piracy and maritime terrorism—including boardings at sea, attempted boardings, hijackings, detentions, suicide attacks, and robberies at port or anchorage—remain a very real problem in many areas of the world.

Although the crews of many hijacked ships are held for ransom, others have been thrown overboard by the sea raiders. Some victims are found; others simply disappear. In addition to the cost in lives, the price of piracy is high in economic terms. Estimates of the monetary cost of piracy range as high as $12 billion a year. While the number of reported attacks is high—and has been growing—the actual count appears to be even higher. In 2009, more than 200 vessels were attacked in the Somalia region alone. The number is likely on the low side. Many ship's masters and owners discourage seamen from reporting pirate attacks, apparently because of the delays that the vessel may encounter as reporting formalities are completed.

Some sea criminals are simple local fishermen who supplement their income by occasional piratical attacks. They hit weak-appearing targets of opportunity. This happened many times to those unfortunate targets known as "boat people" who escaped the bonds of the newly formed Vietnamese government after the fall of Saigon in 1975, only to have their vessels boarded by piratical fishermen and others. These unfortunates lost their few worldly possessions—and sometimes their lives.

As a result of having no effective government during recent years—and with no prospect of improvement, despite years of support and aid—Somali pirates have made piracy a lucrative livelihood, probably the only lucrative business in their violent land. A few short years ago, the Malacca Strait—the narrow stretch of water running between Malaysia and the Indonesian island of Sumatra—was the piracy area *de jour*. Without question, the maritime region off the coast of Somali has become the new danger area. In fact, the attackers there have not only become more emboldened, the international community is spending tens of millions per month trying to patrol this region to deter some of the surge. The costly effort might be improving the situation over what it could be, but it is hardly proving to be a spectacular success. The hijacking and subsequent ransoming of both vessels and crews still occurs frequently. Hardly a week goes by without some piratical act—or several attacks—taking place in the area.

While pirates appear to be motivated largely by money, on the other end of the scale are the trained terrorists who want to hold people hostage or destroy expensive vessels and kill their crews in order to make a sociopolitical statement. And even this field is evolving in light of current events.

A disturbing trend in maritime terrorism is the growing involvement of terrorist groups in the lucrative piracy business. In April 2011, the head of the U.S. military command in Africa—the world's most piracy-prone area—told the U.S. Congress that Somalia's al-Shabaab insurgent movement and an affiliate of al-Qaida is getting some of its money through piracy. He said that it was inevitable that the pirates and al-Qaida will develop a direct link as well. That development, if it hasn't already happened, would give al-Qaida a major funding boost.

While commercial vessels have been the primary targets for pirates in the past few years, yachts are proving to be particularly

The size of your vessel doesn't matter. Oil tanker, fishing vessel, yacht: pirates capture them all. Here, the crew of the Chinese fishing vessel *Tian Yu 8* can be seen gathered on the bow under the guard of pirate gunmen. (U.S. Navy photo)

attractive to seagoing raiders. Several yachts have been taken in the Somali area and those aboard held for ransom—a ransom that often cannot be paid because the yacht owners may have most of their money tied up in their craft.

Yachts are attractive targets because the crews, if any, are small, and those aboard are seldom prepared to defend themselves. Yachts are generally slower than commercial vessels and lower in the water, making it easier for the attackers to overcome resistance and board.

Most important of all considerations, yachts—ton for ton—usually have exceptionally large amounts of cash, salable equipment, and things of value aboard. As an example, in August 1996, four pirates using a small *pedalo*, or pedal-powered dinghy, and wielding a handgun attacked a British yacht and robbed six French passengers of cash and jewelry worth thousands of dollars. Italian media said the yacht *Renalo* was moored off the coast of Calabria in the toe of the boot of Italy, having arrived at the seaside town of Scilla just hours before the bandits struck. One report said the pirates had asked a lifeguard at the beach if they could rent his *pedalo*, threatening him with a pistol when he refused. Then they paddled out and drew alongside the 272-foot (34-meter) yacht, which was moored only hundreds of yards from the shore. They boarded it and tied up the six crew and six passengers. Police said the pirates stole the equivalent of $2,600 in currency and pocketed jewelry worth thousands of dollars more. The thieves then made off in an inflatable powerboat that had been stolen earlier and was brought to the scene of the crime by an accomplice.

But the trend in assaults on pleasure craft is shifting from robbery of valuables to hostage taking for ransom. And it's becoming a deadlier game. In February 2011, four Americans were seized, then slain, by pirates aboard their yacht, *Quest*, even as negotiators tried to reach a deal. Negotiators aboard the USS *Sterett*, standing nearby the yacht several hundred miles south of Oman, were trying to come to an agreement when a pirate sent an RPG whizzing at the American warship. Then volleys of fire broke out on the seized yacht, sending U.S. special forces rescuers pelting to the vessel. At some point the pirates shot the hostages before rescuers could arrive. Two of the pirates were killed in the boarding and two more were found dead, apparently killed by their own in a dispute.

Two days after that slaughter at sea, a Danish family of five—including three children ages 12 to 16—and two crewmembers were accosted by pirates while sailing their yacht in the Indian Ocean and held for $5 million ransom. A later rescue attempt by forces from Puntland failed amid pirate threats that the five, including the children, would be killed in any such attempt.

Even cruise ships are not immune. In 1985, a team of Palestinian terrorists answering to Abul Abbas hijacked the *Achille Lauro*. While Abbas claimed his gunmen only intended to use the cruise liner as a means to slip into Israel, not to commandeer the vessel, that was not how things worked out. His hijackers shot an elderly, infirm American in his wheelchair and tossed his body overboard, and they held more than 300 passengers hostage off Port Said, Egypt, for two days before surrendering to Egyptian authorities.

Egypt, unwilling to deal with the problematic pirates, immediately shipped off Abbas and his men to Tunisia, where he was headquartered. Incensed, the U.S. government sent navy fighters after the plane the hijackers were fleeing on and forced the flight down in Sicily. Italy, in yet another demonstration of the continued unwillingness of even Western governments to deal with piratical killers, then freed Abbas. The Italians allowed him to flee to Yugoslavia before the American arrest warrant for piracy and hostage taking could be served. This unwillingness or inability of government to cope with the piracy problem—leaving the troubles on the doorstep of every captain and seaman—is a worldwide phenomenon.

Every bit as disturbing as the *Achille Lauro* incident was the November 5, 2005, attack on the cruise ship *Seaborne Spirit* about 100 miles off the coast of Somalia. Passengers were awakened to the sights and sounds of three small pirate vessels whose occupants were shooting at the ship with automatic weapons and rocket-propelled grenades (RPGs). The ship's captain turned, dodged, and weaved, but the attackers—whether they were interested in capturing and holding the 151 well-to-do passengers for ransom is unknown—held on. They were finally driven off by a sound-emitting device.

More than two years later, in April of 2008, attackers went after the *Le Ponant*, again near Somalia. It was the turn of those aboard the *Nautica* sailing in the Gulf of Aden in November of that same year. A few days later, in December of 2008, the *Athena* came under fire, and just a day after that, pirates tried again in the Gulf of Aden when they attacked the *Astor*. In April of 2009, it was bad luck of those aboard the *Melody* to face pirates in the Gulf of Aden. In January of 2011, the *Spirit of Adventure* came under attack—again off Somalia in the Gulf of Aden.

Cruise liners are a difficult target because of their speed and a high freeboard that makes boarding problematic. If pirates ever get aboard one, however, the payoff could be tremendous. They have the potential to rob passengers, as lined out in the novel and movie *Assault On a Queen*, or kill them, as the Palestine Liberation Front terrorists did to wheelchair-bound Leon Klinghoffer aboard the *Achille Lauro*, or demand ransom from the families of several hundred seized passengers with enough money to sail a luxury liner.

Somali pirates are now increasing the price for releasing hijacked vessels and crews to several million dollars. Such higher ransoms may induce not only more Somalis but others outside the region to take up piracy. For the most part, the price of a hijacked ship off Somalia was under $1 million in 2007; in 2008 and 2009, it was between $1 and $2 million. At the end of 2009 and beginning of 2010, ransom figures began to escalate to between $2.5 to $5 million.

There are indicators that suggest pirates now expect $10 million for a ship and crew—and sometimes get that amount. While a few

A captured ship's crew surrounded by Somali pirates brandishing AK-47s and RPGs. The crewmembers now must wait for the shipping company to pay the ransom, which can take months of negotiation. (U.S. Navy photo)

years ago the pirates—the gunsels—took their share of the ransom money (perhaps half a million dollars a pop in 2005) and went home to build a palatial mansion for themselves and their family, the increase in revenue has allowed piracy to be conducted on a more businesslike basis, with syndicates financing a planned operation based on spy work in ports and distributing the extra profits to shareholders in the operation.

Actual figures are hard to obtain, because shipping companies are traditionally secretive about the size of ransoms. While the victims tend to keep the payoff price secret, the word about a higher ransom spreads quickly among the piratical community and creates an expectation that in the next takeover, the attackers should get at least the higher amount and perhaps more.

The total ransoms paid for ships and crews were about a quarter billion dollars in 2010, according to some estimates. But the cost of the maritime depredations is far more than just the ransom amounts. Extra costs include millions of dollars in naval expenses for ships and crews of the countries trying to provide protection, and an amount estimated at a shade under $2.5 billion in additional transportation costs for any commodities aboard ships that have to divert to longer routes to avoid the most dangerous areas off Africa.

In fact, everybody pays. Even if the captains and crews undergo the worst treatment of all, the consumer who buys the higher-priced goods carried on those ships is every bit as much a victim as the hijacked crewmember or the insurance company that pays the ransom.

One element that is missing, and badly needed, is coordinated responses. At this point, shipping companies and insurance firms share very little information. There are indications that this may be changing, but at the moment, insurance and shipping companies are only at the talking stage. They need to get to the action stage. When a vessel falls to piracy, the existence of a central registry of what is happening and an exchange of information between companies, where there is agreement to go only so far and no further in payments, could at least stem the ransom appreciation.

In the longer term, international cooperation—both in relation to an agreement to use force to stop hijackings and to punish hijackers—is needed.

There are at least half a dozen ideas being floated to solve the piracy problem through court proceedings. Among them is a proposal to create an international court, under the auspices of the United Nations, to try suspected pirates. While many consider that the most promising of the lot, other proposals involve some sort of court and trial arrangement in other states, or assistance to Somalia to help it prosecute piracy suspects on home territory under Somali law.

The proposals, however well meaning, fail to address a number of issues that work against prosecution of pirates anywhere. There was a reason why governments used to simply swing pirates from the yardarm immediately upon their capture, after brief seaborne trials.

Speedy justice has always been needed—not necessarily because of bloodthirsty vengeance but for a more pragmatic reason: in commercial shipping, time is essential. Captains and crew of vessels attacked by pirates don't stay in port for trials that may take years—neither ship owners nor sailors can afford that. And the ship, crews, and officers cannot be called back to court easily. They are probably three seas and an ocean away when landlubber courts eventually convene. Any proposal that fails to change the rules of evidence—specifically, allowing testimony to be taken at a distance—will fail to solve the problem.

The proposals to tame piracy also never seem to touch the sponsors of maritime terror—the land-based financiers, bankers, spokesmen, support groups, and maritime spy groups that make the actual attacks both possible and profitable.

At the same time, there are differences, internationally, in the definition of piracy or the evidence required to convict a pirate. Everyone knows what a pirate is, but nuances in legal definitions can destroy even the most obvious case. The differences between the way the Russian, Chinese, U.S., and Finnish navy handle pirates they capture can be significant.

Until issues such as these are resolved, a truly international response is impossible. And pirates can sail through the legal and jurisdictional waves with a middle finger in the air—the symbol of piracy that has replaced the Jolly Roger.

As the world dithers, the pirates do not. They continually improve their attack styles and their capabilities. The use of small, high-speed craft has become more prevalent, and boardings have increased worldwide. The pirates often take to sea in mother craft carrying speedboats, small skiffs, or even rowboats with outboard motors. A consistent mark of pirate vessels is the presence of boarding ladders and a stock of AK-47s or grenade launchers. The pirates board passing ships and sail them to anchorages that effectively put them beyond the reach of maritime law enforcement. It is not unusual for Somali-area pirates to hold a score of ships, and 300 or more crewmembers, for ransom in their no-go anchorages.

Once captured, the ship is taken to an anchorage off the Somali coast. Note pirate skiffs alongside and boarding ladder. (U.S. Navy photo)

As noted above, powerful syndicates are springing up—money men and other organizers who provide the weapons and pirate vessels initially, giving the young men who carry out the deed a "job opportunity." It has become big business, with syndicate planners selling shares in preplanned attacks to on-shore investors. In the most plotted-out plans, a pirate syndicate will seize a ship, fraudulently reflag it (generally from some Central American or Caribbean country, where flags of convenience are a big moneymaker), and sell it off to an unsuspecting buyer (or at least a purchaser who will look the other way if he suspects anything). Some of the vast millions of dollars the Somali pirates are receiving are going to provide better boats, equipment, and, most of all, weapons.

Unlike the share-and-share-alike piracy of old, the new business model for piracy means that contributors are paid based on what they bring to the mission—skill sets based on experience, or tangible items such as weapons and equipment. Somalia has been a failed state for about two decades, and the cash from piracy is one of the few ways its inhabitants can make money. Most of the money is parceled out among financiers, negotiators, and local militia leaders. The "hard men"—the attackers of the vessels and guards who watch the captives once the ships and captive crew are brought to shore—often receive a relatively minor cut of between $10,000 and $15,000 each. But that is a fortune in their drug-glazed eyes.

There is a disturbing trend toward the use of firearms and heavier weaponry. Modern-day pirates are bolder in their actions than they were only a decade ago and no longer content themselves indulging in petty thefts with small arms and knives. Somali pirates today do not hesitate to spray target vessels with AK-47 and RPG fire to force their compliance. Such barrages are common "shots across the bow" of everything from fishing vessels and yachts to cargo vessels and cruise liners.

Pirates' proclivity for physical, often gratuitous violence—even after a ship has been boarded and the pirates are in firm control—seems to be growing as well. As far back as 1996, the authoritative

Regional Piracy Center (RPC) of the International Maritime Bureau (IMB) reported: "There is no doubt that attacks on vessels have become more audacious, more violent and an issue of serious concern to shipping and seamen."

That comment is becoming more familiar and ominous each year. Despite the intensive naval patrols and operations by up to five-dozen nations, the number and intensity of attacks is mounting, not diminishing. In the first quarter of 2011, there were more than 140 attacks reported, eclipsing the record for the most attacks in that quarter since statistical collection began in 1991. In that short period, seven mariners were murdered by pirates, 34 were injured, and almost 344 new hostages were taken by individual pirates and their syndicates.

According to IMB officials, "Modern piracy is violent, bloody and ruthless. It is made all the more fearsome because its victims know they are alone and defenseless."

In both Sri Lanka and the Philippines, paramilitary forces of rebels have hijacked large boats as part of their operations. Until 2009, when they were finally defeated after decades of civil war, the Sri Lankan rebel naval force the Sea Tigers, as the guerrillas were known, operated in "wolf packs" of high-speed fiberglass dinghies. Their boats were powered by multiple outboard motors capable of reaching speeds in excess of 30 knots. The craft had mounted guns and rocket launchers. Each boat usually carried five or six terrorist fighters, and, en masse, they were formidable opponents. Even aircraft and government patrol craft had a hard time operating against the Sea Tigers when they moved as a large force. In addition, several Middle Eastern terrorist groups—backed by what many consider to be an outlaw government—have their own naval forces capable of operating against civilian shipping or undefended pleasure craft.

There is a growing body of evidence that suggests portions of ransom money from hijackings is being used to fund terrorists and other non-state actors with a political agenda. Confidential reports

In such crowded ports as Ho Chi Minh City, Viet Nam, the crew must be on the lookout for theft and stowaways. Maritime security is not always about piracy. (Jim Gray photo)

suggest this is true off both the east and west coasts of Africa and to a lesser extent in the Philippines. (The Islamist separatist group Abu Sayyaf in the southern Philippines, for example, is active in maritime terrorism and piracy.) The extent of any funding of these groups is a matter of conjecture, but some reports provide anecdotal evidence of financial ties.

Stowaways are another type of seagoing incident that, while not traditionally thought of as piracy, can be costly to the vessel owner or corporation. One or more individuals will sneak aboard the ship or yacht as it sails away from port. Once aboard, the stowaway becomes the responsibility of the vessel and its owner. The price of returning the stowaway, in terms of money, time, and legal costs, can be significant in many countries. Officials at the next port of call can discover the stowaway and force the vessel to bear all costs of prosecution as well as getting the stowaway back to the earlier port. Shipmasters and owners may even face legal actions for allowing the incident to have occurred.

Clearly, the crews of high-value targets need to be trained how to protect themselves and their vessels against a broad range of threats—from stowaways to political terrorists. Captains need to be well versed in—and willing to employ—techniques that will discourage intruders from boarding in the first place: prevention, if you will. And if attacked, the captain and crew need to be capable of repelling the marauders with minimal casualties to themselves and minimal damage to the vessel.

A quality-trained crew and captain are simply good investments. Whether the vessel is a mega-yacht, a merchantman, or a passenger cruise liner, the owner spends a large amount of money for the initial outlay, as well as a significant amount on an ongoing basis for everything from hull insurance to a well-stocked larder and fine wine list to bottom scraping, fuel, and salaries for the seamen. For relatively little additional cost, owners can have crews trained and vessels outfitted to best prevent or deter acts of piracy, terrorism, and unauthorized boarding. A well-versed and alert crew can hold off attackers under all but the most difficult and dangerous of situations.

EVALUATING THE THREAT

AN OVERVIEW OF PIRACY

Pirates are not benign character actors or electronically operated dummies in an amusement park ride. They never have been anything other than maritime criminals whose propensity for violence made them feared rather than respected.

Pirates acquired a golden sheen from novelists and filmmakers over the last few dozen decades—people who no longer had to face these devilish denizens of the sea. Yet in millennia past, the written record shows that pirates were specialists in violence, fear, and torture. That is why from the earliest historical times, piracy was considered a crime of universal jurisdiction—captured pirates could be and were punished virtually on the spot. Legal niceties were set aside when pirates set aside the law of the sea.

Modern pirates who demand multimillions in ransoms are every bit as violent as their predecessors. The threat to kill their captives if their demands are not met is nothing less than mental torture—for the victims and their loved ones and friends. The physical manhandling of men, women, and children who fall into the scurvy hands of pirates amounts to actual torture.

Yet in today's Sargasso Sea of legal entanglements, nuances make the pirate personality a confused one. Some, particularly defense attorneys, want to paint pirate suspects in colors that glow like a sunset at sea. When the crew of an American warship captured a pirate gang that apparently mistook their frigate for a commercial vessel and fired on them in the Gulf of Aden, the sea lawyers got busy. Dredging up an obscure passage from the early 1800s, they claimed the attackers did not commit an act of piracy because they had not been able to board or rob the warship!

Novel piracy stories—and theories—have now gone from Treasure Island to court filings.

A BRIEF HISTORY

Piracy, one of the oldest professions in the world, results from conditions on land, from decisions made on land. Throughout history, pirates have operated when maritime security forces, whether ancient triremes or massive battle groups composed of carriers and support vessels, are scarce or governments are too scared to take on pirates.

Piracy against seagoing commerce is an ancient activity. The Egyptians, Greeks, Carthaginians, and Romans all faced piracy problems. So long as they provided a strong naval presence, piracy was kept in check. When their naval forces faltered or disappeared, piracy developed new legs.

In the 17th and 18th centuries, ferocious European land

The romantic image of a pirate, as depicted in countless books and films. In reality, pirates were cruel, violent criminals of the seas, and they remain so today. (image © iStockphoto.com/Keith Bishop)

The captured Saudi tanker *Sirius Star* with pirate skiffs tied astern. Its shipping company paid a huge ransom for ship and crew. This common practice only encourages more pirate attacks. (U.S. Navy photo)

wars led countries to build up their armies at the expense of their navies, but the rulers found a work-around to attack their enemy's merchant shipping, which was the source of national wealth and prosperity. In the absence of strong naval forces, governments issued "letters of marque" that gave license to private shipping to attack their enemy's vessels. Many mariners took advantage of this route—but when the fighting in Europe ended, they did not stop their depredations.

Off the coasts of the New World, where governments and naval powers were as weak as a failed state, pirates congregated. In northern Africa, where the leaders looked the other way, the Barbary Corsairs used their land bases as pirate havens. Over several centuries, they found that there was value in live merchant seamen—as slaves if no one would ransom them, or as a human object for barter or sale.

Piracy was largely wiped out in the first third of the 19th century, when trading nations began building and sailing fleets to protect their seaborne commerce against all enemies. The navies of the world, more by accident than design, minimized piracy over most sea lanes by their mere presence for more than a hundred years.

Piracy returned with violent flourish off the coast of Vietnam when the South Vietnamese government fell in 1975. Conditions were ripe: the huge naval forces that had previously sailed the area left, the new government was busy trying to establish its rule on land, and a crop of targets emerged on the high seas. Thousands of South Vietnamese refugees, fleeing by boat to non-Communist destinations, were attacked. The fortunate only lost all their possessions to the seagoing thugs. Many—no one knows how many, as boats and people just disappeared—were killed. Many women were raped. And the lack of a strong seagoing presence allowed the pirates to continue with their depredations.

The downfall of the Soviet Union and the virtual mothballing of that fleet, coupled with a severe cutback in the U.S. Navy's war fleet, opened up new areas for pirates to exploit. The Strait of Malacca—a narrow choke point with different countries on each side, and where there were few naval patrols and many isolated islands that pirates could stage from—boomed with piratical attacks in the 1980s and 1990s. Attackers would climb aboard vessels as they were underway and steal from the cargo or even force the captain to open his safe so they could steal any money in there.

A combination of stiffer patrols and an earthquake that ravaged the pirates' land bases and destroyed their boats eventually brought the attacks there to more manageable proportions. But that didn't happen until Malacca Strait pirates reinvented the Barbary pirates techniques of kidnapping and made piracy much more profitable than it had been. They would board a vessel and take the captain and some other crewmember hostage, steal the ship's papers so they would know who to demand a ransom from, and wait for the money—$50,000 was a typical amount—to be delivered.

That tactic was the foundation upon which pirates off Somalia built. Where pirates in the Malacca Strait didn't have a place they could stash vessels and crews while they negotiated for the ransom payments, Somalia was a country without government or police, a place where ships and crews could be taken and held—much as in the days of the Barbary Corsairs. With no effective central government, Somali pirates didn't need to worry about attack on the landward side of their lairs. At the same time, the navies of the world could not, or would not, enter Somali territorial waters to stop the attacks, punish the attackers, or rescue crew and craft. The pirates found they had the perfect king's X—nonexistent government on the land side, an invisible but absolute barrier on the water side.

At first, attacks off Somalia were sporadic and were reported only near the coast, but escalating ransoms for ship and crew allowed some of the pirates to buy better, speedier, longer-range boats, as well as modern technology such as global positioning systems and improved weaponry. Pirates began ranging hundreds of miles off the coast of Somalia, attacking mercilessly and swiftly moving their victimized vessels and crew into Somali ports where they could not be touched. Everything from yachts to supertankers has been attacked, and ransoms

The dhow is a medium-sized native craft that is a common sight from India to Yemen. Once captured by Somali pirates, the dhow becomes the pirate mother ship due to its greater range. (U.S. Navy photo)

are demanded under the pain of death.

A loosely organized international naval fleet cut back the attacks somewhat, but when pirates began building mansions in Somalia and nearby countries with their ransomed loot, the number of attackers increased exponentially. When less than 1 percent of pirates ever face punishment of any kind, and there is a 99 percent assurance of relatively great wealth, the temptation becomes the act.

Modern piracy remains a "for profit" activity. But there is concern at some levels that the practice will morph into a modern mixture of letters of marque attacks, maritime crime, and terrorism. (See "Maritime Terrorism" section below.)

FIVE SCENARIOS OF MODERN PIRACY

Today there are five common piracy scenarios.

In the simplest version, the pirates simply steal from the ship or rob the crew and then depart over the side. Most often this occurs when the victim vessel is at anchor in a port or roadstead. Some consider this penny-ante crime, but attacks like this can easily result in injury or death for anyone aboard a merchant vessel or the owners, passengers, and crew of yachts. In the days before the "peace dividend," the fall of the Soviet Union, and the castration of both the Soviet and American fleets, this was the most prevalent type of maritime crime.

In the second type of piracy, often identified with historical pirate attackers like Blackbeard in the Caribbean waters, the thieves target the entire cargo, or the people, aboard the victimized vessel rather than looking for a few expensive possessions and pocket change. Cargo can be resold, quite often on the black market, and people killed or set adrift. In some cases, the craft—if it is not unique or highly unusual— can be repainted, altered, renamed, and provided with false papers. The vessel can then be sold to an unsuspecting or purposely blind buyer in some port far from the scene of the attack. In these types of cases, the pirates generally try to leave no witnesses to the takeover.

A third type of attack is one in which pirates buy or take over a vessel, reflag it, and then run a "phantom ship" operation that hijacks the cargo of anyone foolish enough to consign goods to the vessel. The pirates may also use the vessel to haul illicit drugs or other contraband. The phantom ship trick involves sophisticated gangs who have been known to steal more than $200 million per year worth of cargo. Many of the ships are flagged in Central American ports. Phantom ships take aboard cargo that is easily disposed of but not easily traced, such as timber, metals, and minerals. Although yacht owners seldom face the phantom ship scenario, its significance lies in pointing out that masters and crew must be prepared to deal with people who are capable of thinking. A defense against sheer thuggery is not enough.

The fourth type has become the scenario *de jour*. The ship is boarded and hijacked, most often while underway. The pirates subdue the crew and take over the vessel, which is sailed to the pirate's lair and held. The pirates notify the ship's owner that they can get the ship and crew released for X millions of dollars. Negotiations take place and generally after a number of months, a settlement is reached, ransom is paid, and the ship released with the crew. The cost of insuring against such a scenario was once thought to be the value of the release of the

The captured Chinese fishing vessel *Tian Yu 8* with pirates in control. The pirates can hold a ship of this size for ransom or use her as a mother ship, forcing her crew to work for them. (U.S. Navy photo)

ship and its cargo. But under the new twist of this scenario, the human value of the crew is often added into the equation.

The fifth type of pirate attack—harkening back to the days when European countries issued letters of marque to civilian vessels to attack an enemy's shipping—is more a political/social event than an economic one: the attackers seek to destroy a vessel and its cargo to affect governments and markets. Attacking tankers with their expensive cargoes in choke points to bottle up other vessels exemplifies this type of attack. It is still rare, but it could become more prevalent—and far more costly to the world—than any of the types of attacks found today.

PIRACY-PRONE REGIONS

Although piracy is endemic and pervasive in some areas, attacks can happen almost anywhere. Regions without a history of attacks can suddenly find themselves scupper-deep in seaborne raiders.

Following a years-long downswing, there has been a recent upsurge in pirate attacks in the South China Sea and the Strait of Malacca. Unlike attacks off Africa, where individual countries have no overriding need to halt the maritime depredations, the upsurge in Asian waters threatens China's national security and trade interests. Since about 75 to 80 percent of China's international trade traverses the shipping lanes of the South China Sea and the Strait of Malacca, China will probably move—using both diplomatic and military means—to shut down pirate activity in that area.

The center of piracy today is off Africa's east coast, particularly in the waters off Somalia. While dozens of international warships are mounting antipiracy patrols in the area, they are far too few to cover the Indian Ocean and African coastal regions. There is also the problem of what to do with pirates after they are apprehended. Some are tried locally, some face courts further away, but for a variety of reasons, many suspects are released to return home and try their hand, and guns, again.

More Somali pirates than ever before have been taking to the water, and strategies against them range from installing "safe rooms" aboard commercial vessels to hiring private security escort warships. To this point, no strategy has proven totally successful, in part because the international community and maritime businesses—shipping companies, insurers, etc.—cannot agree on a common plan.

The current international naval presence in the area is likely to become semipermanent, although the size of the force may vary based on economic and political conditions within the contributing countries. In bad economic times, or when a nation is in political ferment, countries often become stingy with their naval assets. At this point, sea patrols by the Contact Group on Piracy—a consortium of 60 countries—cover a million square miles of sea.

Worldwide, a typical month of reported pirate attacks—experts estimate that only about 10 percent of such attacks are reported—might look something like the following listing, based on a U.S. Navy Office of Naval Intelligence transcript that comes out weekly and covers the previous four weeks.

NORTH AMERICA: No current incidents to report.

CENTRAL AMERICA-CARIBBEAN:
    ST. VINCENT AND THE GRENADINES: Catamaran robbed while anchored at Admiral Bay, Princess Point. Vessel was boarded while crew was away. Upon their return, they noticed the sliding door was open and some electronic items were missing. Local police investigated the incident.

SOUTH AMERICA:
    ECUADOR: Reefer vessel robbed while at Puerto Bolivar anchorage. Four robbers armed with guns and knives boarded the vessel from a boat. The robbers were spotted by a member of the ship's crew, who raised the alarm. The robbers attacked the crewmember, forcing him on the deck and then tying him up. Shore security was on the vessel and the

robbers jumped overboard, escaping in a waiting boat along with ship's properties.

ATLANTIC OCEAN AREA: No current incidents to report.

NORTHERN EUROPE—BALTIC: No current incidents to report.

MEDITERRANEAN—BLACK SEA: No current incidents to report.

WEST AFRICA:

GUINEA: Vehicle carrier robbed while berthed in Conakry. Robbers boarded the vessel via the forward mooring ropes and stole ship's stores before escaping.

CAMEROON: Fishing vessel fired upon, one crewmember killed, while underway in the coastal waters off Cameroon and Nigeria. Armed robbers attacked the vessel, injuring eight crewmembers and killing another. The men looted the vessel, taking everything that could be moved, before leaving.

CAMEROON: Seismic survey vessel fired upon while underway, approximately 2NM [nautical miles] off the coast. The vessel, supported by four chase boats with armed personnel onboard, was approached by two boats with six armed men in each. The boats opened fire on one chase boat and attempted to board. The armed guards returned fire and the two boats moved away.

RED SEA:

RED SEA: Bulk carrier reported suspicious approach while underway, approximately 220NM northwest of the Bab el Mandeb. Captain reported seeing two skiffs with seven armed men in each approach the vessel 1NM away. Captain raised the alarm, conducted evasive maneuvers, mustered the crew, and activated fire hoses. The suspicious skiffs continued to follow the vessel for 30 minutes before moving away.

RED SEA: Chemical tanker reported suspicious approach while underway approximately 28NM northwest of Mokha, Yemen. Three skiffs approached the vessel from different directions. Alarm was raised, crew mustered, and the vessel increased speed while conducting evasive maneuvering. The crew also activated hot water curtain and foam monitors. After approximately 40 minutes of pursuit, the skiffs moved away. A helicopter was dispatched to the scene.

RED SEA: Vessel reported suspicious approach while underway approximately 12NM west of Mokha, Yemen. Captain reported five high-speed skiffs approached the vessel to less than 150 meters. Vessel conducted evasive maneuvering and the skiffs eventually moved away.

RED SEA: Bulk carrier reported suspicious approach while underway approximately 70NM southeast of Tio, Eritrea. Two white skiffs approached the vessel, one at the port bow and the other at the starboard bow. The skiff on the port side suddenly increased speed toward the vessel. Once the vessel steered toward the starboard side, the second skiff increased speed as well. The crew was alerted and fire hoses were activated. After approximately 10 minutes, the two skiffs abandoned their pursuit and moved away.

RED SEA: Vessel reported suspicious approach while underway approximately 53NM northeast of Tio, Eritrea. Master reported being approached by one skiff with four persons onboard equipped with two black ladders. No further information to provide.

RED SEA: Container ship reported suspicious approach while approximately 18NM west of Mokha, Yemen. An unlit small boat doing a speed of 17 knots approached the vessel. Vessel increased speed, conducted evasive maneuvers, and activated fire hoses and searchlights. The closest point of approach of the boat was 50 meters before moving away.

RED SEA: Bulk carrier reported suspicious approach while underway approximately 65NM northeast of Tio, Eritrea. Two fishing boats approached the vessel from the starboard side at high speed. The master conducted evasive maneuvers and fired a rocket flare when the boats were 100 meters away. Three more fishing boats were spotted 300 meters away and began approaching at a high speed. The master raised the alarm and continued evasive maneuvering. Two more rocket flares were fired at the boats. The fishing boats eventually moved away from the vessel and headed westward. No fishing equipment was seen on the boats.

RED SEA: Tanker reported suspicious approach while underway in approximately 48NM northwest of Ras Isa, Yemen. Two suspicious boats with six to seven persons onboard each approached the vessel at a distance of about 1NM and then closed to 300 meters. They continued to follow for approximately 10 minutes. The security team onboard activated their LRAD [long-range acoustic device] at the port bridge wing. The master conducted evasive maneuvers using hard to helm tactics. The alarm was raised and the crew mustered at the steering gear room. Shortly after the alarm was heard, the two boats altered course away from the vessel.

RED SEA: Chemical tanker hijacked while underway approximately 18NM west of Mokha, Yemen. Pirates boarded and hijacked the vessel along with its 18 crewmembers.

A typical Somali pirate skiff. It will dash from the mother ship at high speed. When it gets close enough, its crew will display AK-47s and RPGs, threatening the bridge to heave to so they can board. This evolution can take mere minutes, depending on range and compliance from the target vessel. (U.S. Navy photo)

INDIAN OCEAN-EAST AFRICA:

GULF OF ADEN: Chemical tanker fired upon while underway approximately 110NM southwest of Al Mukalla, Yemen. Six men in a skiff, armed with automatic weapons and RPGs, approached the vessel from the starboard beam and started firing. The duty officer raised the alarm and mustered the crew. The vessel increased speed, activated fire hoses, sent out a distress call, and fired rocket flares. A nearby warship was contacted and deployed a helicopter to provided assistance. The armed men eventually ceased firing and aborted the attack. The warship pursued the skiff and was able to apprehend the suspected pirates.

GULF OF ADEN: General cargo ship hijacked while underway approximately 90NM southwest of Al Mukalla, Yemen. Pirates in three skiffs armed with automatic weapons boarded the vessel, taking the 24 crewmembers hostage.

MOZAMBIQUE: Yacht robbed while anchored off Bara Lodge, near Inhambane. Two sailors awoke during the night to find a man with a knife about to cut their fuel line. The robber had already stolen several items when the men became aware of his presence on the boat. One of the men wrestled with the robber, who dropped the knife before jumping back into the water. He stole fishing gear, diesel fuel, clothes, and personal items.

BANGLADESH: Chemical tanker reported attempted boarding at 0330 local time while anchored in Chittagong anchorage. About 17 robbers from two wooden boats attempted to board the vessel. The incident was reported to the Bangladesh Coast Guard.

BANGLADESH: Bulk carrier boarded while berthed at Chittagong anchorage. Four robbers armed with knives boarded the vessel via the stern using ropes. Duty watch spotted the robbers, informed the watch officer, and raised the alarm. The robbers aborted the operation and escaped. Nothing was reported stolen.

PERSIAN GULF: No current incidents to report.

SOUTHEAST ASIA:
>MALAYSIA: Tanker boarded at 0347 local time while approximately 2.5NM east of Pulau Mungging. Three robbers reportedly armed with guns boarded the vessel. The crew

raised the alarm and began searching the vessel for the intruders, who later escaped in a boat. No crewmembers were injured and nothing was reported stolen.

MALAYSIA: Vessel robbed while underway in STS lighting area, Johor port. Crewmembers on deck patrol noticed a small motorboat moving away from the ship's stern. The duty officer on the bridge was immediately informed. Upon inspection, the fire station door was found open and ship's equipment was stolen.

SINGAPORE STRAIT: Tug reported suspicious approach at 0540 local time while anchored approximately 3NM northeast of Horsburgh Lighthouse, Singapore. The master reported two men in a small fast craft approached the vessel at anchor with intent to board. The alert crew spotted the craft and directed searchlights toward it. Upon seeing the crew's alertness, the suspicious craft moved away.

SINGAPORE STRAIT: Bulk carrier boarded at 0330 local time while anchored approximately 7NM northeast off Horsburgh Lighthouse, Singapore. Five men onboard a speedboat armed with guns and knives boarded the vessel using ropes. The duty officer onboard noticed the boarding and sounded the general alarm. No injuries were reported and nothing was stolen.

INDONESIA: Container ship robbed while anchored approximately 9NM north of Belawan port during the night, while robbers boarded the vessel undetected, broke into the paint locker, and stole ship's stores. The crew discovered the theft in the morning.

INDONESIA: General cargo vessel reported attempted boarding at 0200 local time while underway approximately

5NM northeast of Muri Island. Nine robbers attempted to board the vessel underway. The men had secured a line to the vessel when an alert watchman sighted the men and raised the alarm. The duty officer took evasive maneuvers and the robbers aborted the boarding attempt.

PHILIPPINES: Tanker robbed at 0145 local time while anchored Batangas anchorage. Three robbers in a small craft approached the vessel at anchor. One robber boarded the vessel and broke into the bosun store. The alert crew spotted the robber and raised the alarm. Upon seeing the crew's reaction, the robber jumped overboard and escaped. A second robber climbing the anchor chain also escaped. Ship's property was stolen. Coast guard was informed.

NORTH ASIA: No current incidents to report.

PACIFIC-ANTARCTIC OCEAN: No current incidents to report.

Studying three or four months of piracy reports provides a good look at where incidents have been *reported*. Considering that only a small percentage of such incidents are reported, the fact that no or few reports come from a given area is no proof that there aren't problems.

Nonreporting is endemic in the maritime community for a number of reasons. Most often, ships are sailing on a schedule. An investigation into an incident may take days to complete. The ship will be held in port while the investigation continues, throwing off the sailing schedule. Ship owners and captains would rather absorb the loss to pirates than lose days to police forces.

It is not uncommon for victims of maritime crime to suspect—often with good reason—that the very people they would ask to investigate the incident are those who carried it out. Waterfront corruption, and law enforcement or maritime police involvement in crime, is not unheard of. No positive results are to be expected when asking the criminals to investigate themselves.

And there is always a jurisdiction problem. If maritime attackers are caught, which jurisdiction will prosecute them? Will it be the local authorities if the crime occurred in a port? In international waters, will it be the courts of the country that flagged the ship, courts in the country where the arresting party came from, authorities at the nearest port? Jurisdictional problems for a trial—and the cost to a government of imprisoning a maritime marauder—mean that most countries would rather not deal with the problem.

Because a country or area is not listed in reports as being problematic is no reason to assume that it is safe.

Though Peru was not considered one of the traditional hotbeds of piracy, in June 1998, pirates attacked a score of Peruvian fishing vessels. The raiders would shoot in on speedboats from Ecuadorian waters to prey on the fishing vessels. The ski-masked and heavily armed pirates boarded their hapless, helpless targets to steal everything of value, including electronics and the fish catches. At least a dozen fishermen were reported injured in the series of boardings.

Iranian waters aren't usually listed among the most dangerous either, but in Tehran, in July 1998, the Iranian police report allegedly broke up a network of pirates. The thieves robbed and killed crews of commercial craft operating in the Gulf. Using speedboats, the pirates reportedly intercepted vessels moving cargoes of cigarettes between Iranian ports and other Gulf harbors, killing 11 people during their depredations.

European waters are not noted for pirates, but recall the August 1996 attack of the British yacht *Renalo* off the Calabrian coast. Four pirates using a small pedal-powered dinghy and wielding a handgun robbed six French passengers of cash and jewelry worth thousands of dollars.

They were lucky. Occasionally yacht attacks have an even sadder ending. The yacht *Carenia* was riding quietly at anchor in a Corfu cove on September 27, 1996, when four attackers in a speedboat pulled alongside about midnight. The owner of the yacht, Keith Hedley, woke up and attempted to foil the marauders with a shotgun blast. His too-little, too-late effort came to naught; Hedley and three friends were held at gunpoint while the pirates ransacked the yacht for valuables. The shotgun blast, though it didn't hold off the pirates, brought police pelting out. They drew up while the pirates were still aboard the *Carenia*. Hedley was fatally wounded during the ensuing gunfight between police and pirates. And the pirates escaped.

The Caribbean region can be problematic, but not to the extent of the roiling, boiling waters off Africa and the Indian Ocean. Still, incidents do occur there, such as the catamaran robbery listed above, or an April 2011 episode where a fishing vessel was robbed while anchored off of Montrose, Guyana, by four armed bandits.

The world leaders in pirate attacks in the mid-1990s were the same six countries that have historically shared the distinction. The

The Malacca Strait of Southeast Asia. The presence of many small islands and lots of native craft make it a pirate haven. Pirates dash out on a yacht or ship operating in its restricted waters or at anchorage. (Jim Gray photo)

six—the sites of more than half of the recorded attacks—were Indonesia, Thailand, Brazil, the Philippines, Sri Lanka, and India. Of those six, the region in and around the Malacca Strait contained the most incidents.

The new wave of piracy has largely shoved those perennial pirate havens into relative obscurity. In a couple of decades, losses from the "average" maritime piracy event skyrocketed from a few hundred dollars in equipment and cargo, to $50,000 ransoms of a ship's captain and other officers in Indonesian waters, to multimillion dollar ransoms of crew, ship, and cargo off Somalia and adjacent waters. The price continues to rise, and there is no apparent end. What the traffic will bear is the price now.

Since about 2000, the Somali coastline has become the single most pirate-infested waterway in the world. Those waters claim more incidents now—and more lives—than attacks in all the world's seas combined. Pirate activity in the Gulf of Aden and Indian Ocean off Somalia's east coast often picks up after periods of poor weather that kept pirates in port or unable to launch from mother ships, and after a hijacked ship has been ransomed, thereby releasing a pirate gang to go out to hunt ships again.

There is a legitimate fear that the tactics practiced and perfected by Somali pirates will become the blueprint for increasing piracy in many other nations and waters. This is because the booty is counted in the multimillions per year. Despite a multinational seaborne effort by the more than nine navies concentrated in stopping the piracy in this area, little has been done to deter the acts occurring almost daily in that region.

LOCATIONS OF PIRATE ATTACKS

Modern pirates, as in the past, come in three types. There is the purely criminal variety, the semiofficial military variety, and the terrorist type. The last type may have had military special operations training. The terrorist type may be the most difficult to deal with, but all three types need to be reckoned with in many areas of the world.

The location of the attack—the area of the world and the type of waterway where the attack occurs—often dictates the type of pirate that a captain and crew are likely to encounter and the level of violence they can expect.

Pirate attacks happen in the following areas:

- The open ocean
- Restricted waterways
- Anchorages
- Pierside

Open Ocean

Open ocean attacks on large vessels while underway usually require a trained team to assure success. Somali pirates are the premier example of a modern-day pirate crew that have demonstrated incredible flexibility to adapt new tactics and techniques, and the willingness to employ new equipment, to succeed at their trade.

Open ocean attacks on small defenseless craft, like the attacks perpetrated against the boat people of Vietnam, may have been carried out by relative amateurs. Historically, those attackers preferred to leave no tattletales alive. The rule was: "If you are going to kill anyone, kill everyone. Leave no witnesses." It is only recently that the pirates have learned the value of keeping the vessel crews hostage until a ransom can be negotiated and paid.

It is important to note that piracy on the open ocean, though it occurs on water, is land-based. Modern pirates do not live their lives at sea. They have quarters ashore and use land-based facilities to provide stores, tools of the trade, and the information that makes them effective. To understand piracy, to combat pirates and maritime marauders, and to protect a vessel and crew from the ravages of piracy, requires a superior knowledge of the land as well as the water.

Narrow Waterways

Canal channels, rivers, straits, harbors, or any narrow waterways are often prime targeting areas for the second type of pirate attack. The targeted vessels are physically forced through narrow channels that restrict both their maneuverability and the options they have to avoid pirates. The Strait of Malacca, between the island-studded coastlines of Malaysia and Indonesia, is one of the best-known locations for narrow waterway attacks. Here, once the pirates have attacked their victims, they can easily disappear into well over 10,000 island lairs. There are examples of this narrow waterway type of attack even in the United States, where small ships and crews navigating the rivers and bayous between Florida and Louisiana can be victimized. The American pirates sometimes use small craft but in many cases will even attack moored boats from land. A land-launched attack gives them speed, mobility, and ease of escape over the well-developed road system.

Today, activity in the relatively narrow passage off Somalia has shown that it's not safe to sail through this region. But new tactics employing the use of a mother vessel from which to stage the smaller raiding boats has permitted the pirates to extend their nefarious trade well off the coastline and into the open seas. Not only are some of these daring pirates operating hundreds of miles off the coastline, but most recently they seem to be extending their operations down off the east coast of Africa as far south as Kenya and Madagascar.

Anchorages

Moorages and anchorages can become prime pirate areas. Even vessels that are rafted up and moored alongside one another are not immune. Pirates find the approach is easy in an anchorage. Sitting snugly in what they consider a safe harbor or roadstead, ships' crews are generally relaxed and unsuspecting. Small craft are around all the time. The close approach of a boat may be mentally unnoted, even if the craft is seen. At night the pirates may use stealth and darkness as a cover while drifting down on the target from a screen of vessels in the vicinity.

Theft in broad daylight. One of the authors photographed these guys as they boldly lowered bikes and other gear off this ship while the crew was nowhere in sight. (Jim Gray photo)

Once pirates have successfully attacked a target in moorages and anchorages, they disappear into the maze of the surrounding vessels or return to a nearby port facility, where they remove the spoils and easily dispose of them on the black or gray market. Vessels are seldom hijacked in this type of attack—getting the ship underway is usually beyond the pirates' capabilities. These attackers usually want things they can carry away, not the ship and its cargo.

Pierside

Pierside attacks are less common. In most instances, the thefts will be relatively petty. Violence is always a possibility; however, the pierside pirate is usually more interested in filching a few items or dollars that he can carry away than he is in physical violence. Pierside attackers don't necessarily use a vessel to approach the target; they can swim or walk to it. Once they have their booty—almost always portable—

they can walk down the gangway and disappear into the maze of shoreline structures. This is territory they are familiar with, among a population they know, in a place where they can fence the stolen valuables or spend the money.

ANATOMY OF A PIRATE ATTACK

Piracy at sea is really nothing more than a seagoing ambush. As such, piracy is a process. All ambushes, whether at sea or ashore, share common traits. The essentials of an ambush remain the same no matter who the attacker may be, no matter who the intended victim is, no matter where it takes place.

An ambush is a surprise attack upon a moving or temporarily halted target with the mission of destroying or capturing the "enemy" or his possessions. The common element of all ambushes is simple: the quarry is moving, or is stopped somewhere while in the process of moving, when a sudden attack unfolds.

Ambushes are characterized by short, intensely violent action followed by complete and rapid withdrawal. The ambush is not intended to extend over a prolonged period. Normally, the pirate/ambusher will inflict the greatest amount of damage in the initial minutes. Every book dealing with ambushes repeats "surprise, surprise, surprise" like some mantra. But the "common knowledge" that surprise is the most essential element in an ambush or pirate attack is fatally flawed. We stress that if there is a single key to a successful ambush, any ambush, it has to be *mobility.* Even more than surprise, mobility is the limiting factor for defender and attacker alike.

Defeating modern pirates depends on understanding their tactics and techniques, avoiding surprise, retaining mobility, and depriving the attacker of mobility.

The ambush process involves a seven-step operational sequence:

* Stalk
* Site

- Stop
- Shock
- Smother
- Secure, Search, and Snatch
- Scram (sometimes with ship)

These seven steps cover, in a general way, all phases of an ambusher's attack—before, during, and after the violence or threat of violence. Every ambush or pirate attack involves these seven steps in some way.

There is no way to affix a time frame to any of the steps. Sometimes a single step in the process may take days or weeks to carry out. In other cases, a step may last no more than a fraction of a second. In the case of three of the steps—stop, shock, and smother—the action takes place virtually simultaneously. In many ambushes or pirate attacks, this trilogy of steps may take less than five minutes from initiation to completion. In some cases of an improvised attack, all of the "ambush essentials" may be carried out in a matter of minutes.

Stalking and siting are pre-ambush phases of the process. Stalking, in a sense, is the intelligence gathering and planning phase. This is where the ambusher finds out, deduces, or decides where and under what circumstances the victim should be ambushed. Pirates use everything from waterfront scuttlebutt about ships, cargoes, and crews to sophisticated communication interception tools in this phase. There are reports that many of the major boardings by Somali pirates have been orchestrated by well-connected criminal gangs located in other countries.

After a vessel has been targeted, pirates will move in closer to get more intelligence to build on their assault plan. A complacent crew will not detect this stakeout. A professionally trained crew has a better chance of detecting the surveillance being conducted against their vessel.

Siting is the process of moving the attackers or the weapons of attack into the proper place for the attack. Maritime choke points such as straits and island chains are ideal for this tactic. Stalking and siting are two points at which pirate attacks should be stopped.

Stop, shock, and smother take place at the ambush site. This trilogy is at the heart of any attack. To be successful, the ambush target must be halted and prevented from going anywhere—especially from escaping. Deception is a common tactic to make the victim stop or allow the pirate to come aboard. Ruses can range from a ship claiming to be in distress and asking for assistance to parading a pretty girl in a bikini around another boat in port. Even a pierside pizza delivery can be used to get aboard. There have been instances where the perpetrator used official uniforms to gain access to the target vessel. Somali pirates have depended on sneaking up behind freighters or tankers, often in the "radar shadow." The pirates board the vessel and then take control. Once pirates are aboard, the ability to halt their takeover diminishes greatly.

Pirates use a variety of diversions, choke points, and screens to get into attack position. They can lay obstacles such as nets or cables. Some will use the low tide in tidal areas to restrict the speed—or even the movement—of craft, attacking in shallow water when deeper drafted vessels cannot move or maneuver. Pirates may also play on Good Samaritan instincts, calling for a vessel to stop to help rescue a "man overboard" or a swimmer in distress.

In what is known as a "swarm" tactic, attackers may approach at high speed, using many boats at the same time, literally overwhelming their prey by the superior numbers of attackers.

In some cases, pirates use multiple vessels operating from a mother ship. While one vessel distracts the crew on the target vessel by coming alongside and shooting RPGs or small arms at it, other boats come up from behind. These pirates board at the stern and quickly move to the bridge to take over the ship.

Smother is the part of the ambush that involves overwhelming any initial resistance. This is the last point at which the crew and passengers on a targeted vessel can have any effect on the outcome. While a pirate attack, or any other ambush, may fail after this point, the failure will usually be due to the intervention of outside forces.

Secure, search, and snatch are the ambush follow-ups—things such

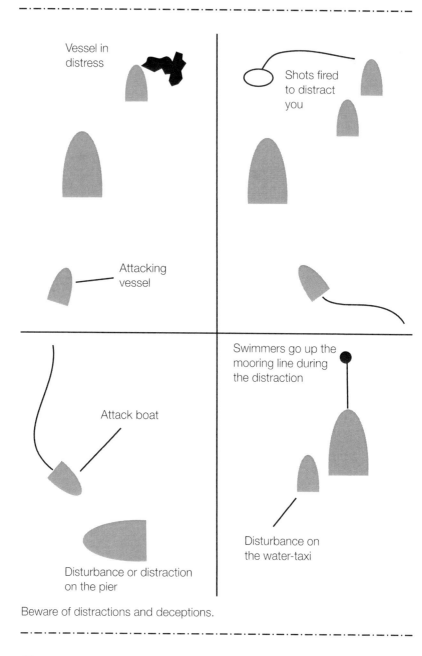

Vessel in distress

Shots fired to distract you

Attacking vessel

Swimmers go up the mooring line during the distraction

Attack boat

Disturbance on the water-taxi

Disturbance or distraction on the pier

Beware of distractions and deceptions.

as making certain that none of the quarry have escaped, searching for weapons or papers, and snatching hostages or materials. This phase, too, takes place at the ambush site.

The last phase of an ambush is scram—a descriptive way to define what the military likes to call exfiltration. The worldlier define this step as "getting the hell out of here." Often, in attacks like those off Somalia, the pirates scram with the ship, captain, and crew.

EVOLVING ANTIPIRACY MEASURES

Some recent developments auger well, provided they are actually carried through and expanded. After more than a decade of neglect, more attention is being paid, belatedly, to the piracy problem by business, governments, and the shipping lines. Typically, conferences today are calling for:

An unexploded RPG warhead embedded in the side of a luxury liner. Pirates have no problems about shooting to make their point! (U.S. Navy photo)

- Continued or upgraded naval response
- Efforts to shut down the financial pipeline
- Arrest, prosecution, and jailing of pirates

There are indications that some governments are abandoning their stand-by-and-watch behavior of past years, increasingly ordering their navies to board vessels under pirate control, even at the risk to captives. This is hardly an across-the-board response, and it may well be reversed because some pirates have killed their hostages in such circumstances. However, if the trend were to continue and all parties understood that rescue missions would be laid on as a matter of course, it would prompt captains to be more judicious where they sailed, crews to be more alert, and everyone to treat a trip through dangerous waters with a back-to-the-wall attitude. Shipping companies, captains, and crews still need to take a more proactive attitude toward their own security in pirate-prone waters. About one in five ships transiting the most dangerous areas still aren't following the "best practices" checklist of things such as increasing the number of lookouts or sailing at high speed to thwart attacks.

There is also some indication that pirates themselves are being prosecuted and jailed with more regularity than in the past, although the probability of escaping capture and incarceration still remains high. According to some estimates, at least three-quarters of active pirates have been taken into custody somewhere along their criminal life, and of those arrested for their maritime attacks, an estimated 80 percent were then set free.

Finally, there is some slight movement toward arresting and prosecuting the shoreward side of the piracy teams—the corrupt port officials; politicos; "investors" from Asia, Europe, and the Americas; negotiators; and money people who receive tens of thousands of dollars for juggling the phone, paperwork, and payment. These people are the backbone of piracy. They pay for upfront costs in high-speed craft, weapons, and GPS equipment. Some will gather information on possible or actual targets from sources that identify insured ships, or identify family members of crew to turn the screws a little tighter. They keep the largest portion of the proceeds, using non-Western money transfer systems to distribute the proceeds among themselves.

When the members of this syndicate can be identified, they can be taken into custody. These people are not usually armed—they consider themselves intellectually superior to the triggermen on the ships and the governments who flag the vessels—and tend toward arrogance rather than slyness. They travel internationally and can often be picked up as they move from country to country. U.S. authorities apprehended one such suspect when he returned to the United States, where he lived. Another suspect was nabbed by FBI agents in Somalia and hustled back to the States for trial.

EVALUATING THE THREAT

MARITIME TERRORISM

Waterway attacks have become a favored tactic of maritime terrorists. Al-Qaeda and its spawn are particularly prone to using suicide attackers against waterborne targets.

In October of 2000, an al-Qaeda suicide attacker's raft approached the USS *Cole*, blowing up as it neared the warship and punching a massive hole in the ship's side. The explosion nearly blasted the *Cole* to the bottom of Aden harbor; only expert damage-control parties kept the ship afloat. The attack killed 17 U.S. sailors and wounded many others. That was the second attempt at a maritime attack on an American warship in the southern Yemen port. An earlier attempt that same year foundered when the weight of the explosives in the suicide raft sank the vessel as it left on its mission.

Two years later, an al-Qaeda attack damaged a French tanker in the Gulf of Aden. The *Limburg* was attacked a few miles off the coast of Aden, and one crewman was killed. That attack, carried out by a small suicide craft packed with explosives, was believed to have been the work of al-Qaeda operatives in Yemen. The *Limburg* was damaged and lost some oil but did not sink

Al-Qaeda apparently refined the design of the attack, but got no better result, with an attempt in the narrow Strait of Hormuz on July 28, 2010. An al-Qaeda linked group calling itself the Abdullah Azzam

The USS *Cole* underway to the Mediterranean Sea, approximately one month before being attacked by a terrorist-suicide mission on 12 October 2000, while refueling in the port city of Aden, Yemen. (U.S. Navy photo)

Brigades claimed the attack on the 333-meter-long *M.Star* supertanker, owned by the Mitsui OSK. The strait, a gateway to the oil-producing Persian Gulf, limits maneuverability and "fixes" maritime targets. At first, no one knew what really happened—early reports ascribed the damage to the tanker as wave-caused—but after an investigation, officials in the United Arab Emirates said the outer hull of the *M.Star* was blasted inward—dented—by homemade explosives carried aboard what was believed to be a suicide bomber's dinghy that approached the tanker. Crewmembers aboard the ship said they saw a flash and heard an explosion, but there were no reports of any boat approaching the tanker. Instead, the ship, loaded with two million barrels of oil, was suddenly hit by a blast that shattered windows, ripped off railings on the deck, and destroyed a lifeboat. One crewman was reported to be slightly injured.

NARROW WATERWAY ATTACKS

Like pirates, terrorists have been known to attack ships in narrow waterways. Attackers use standoff weapons against the craft and its passengers; destruction and death, not robbery, is the aim.

A Muslim fundamentalist campaign to destroy the tourist industry in Egypt in the mid-1990s is a perfect case study of the technique of ambushing watercraft as they move along inland waterways. While many of those attacks failed in every tactical sense, they resulted in a publicity coup, which made them highly successful in the strategic sense. For that reason, they are likely to be repeated by terrorists and rebels elsewhere and are just as important to study as acts of piracy on the open seas.

A History of Violence

Starting in mid-1992, militants in Egypt mounted a highly effective ambush campaign that targeted tourists and the tourist trade. These were the major producers of foreign exchange and the economic mainspring of the country. The militant campaign was as simple as it was effective. The weapons—guns and bombs—were easy to obtain. The targets were unarmed boats and river craft. This inventive ambush campaign, carried out by a handful of people, wrecked the country's tourist industry within a matter of months.

On October 2, 1992, the organization known as Gama'a attacked a Nile cruiser ferrying 140 Germans on a placid cruise along the river. Three Egyptian crewmembers were wounded in that waterway ambush.

On April 9 of the following year, ambushers were back blasting at boats in a revival of riverine ambush. The Gama'a militants fired at a Nile cruiser carrying 41 Germans down the river in the troubled southern province of Asyut, Egypt's chief stronghold of Muslim militants. Nobody was injured—except the tourist industry.

On September 18, gunmen again opened fire on a Nile cruiser carrying 22 French tourists near Asyut. Militants blasted away from positions along the banks of a plantation. They missed, security sources said, but other reports said the ambushers broke one of the craft's windows. The two things everyone seemed to agree on was that no casualties were reported among tourists aboard the ship and that the attackers got a lot of publicity—worldwide notoriety, in fact.

Anatomy of a Narrow Waterway Ambush

Rivers, canals and sloughs, and other restricted waterways all make effective kill zones. An ambush in these locations requires fewer logistics than almost any other common type. Waterway ambushes can be staged with very few to no rockets, small amounts of ammunition, and little or no explosives.

The climate along many waterways is temperate, a factor that favors ambushing forces because they can remain immobile, in place, for lengthy periods of time without experiencing severe discomfort. At the same time, the terrain usually favors using the ambush as a tactic.

Rivers and other narrow waterways present shallow water with restricted passage. A transiting vessel can be in peril of a rapid attack from shore or smaller craft. This photo was taken in Viet Nam. (Jim Gray photo)

Generally, a river has a plethora of locations where cover and concealment can be found. An attacker almost always has clear field of fire. Because rivers are natural channels that widen and narrow, often significantly, they have natural choke points that can be easily exploited.

A good waterway ambush is easiest when the cover afforded by the riverine environment is used well. High banks, trees, islands, and rocks all make excellent cover. Islands, obstructing rocks in the waterway, and bends in the river may channelize boats into waters where maneuverability is restricted. In fact, narrow waterway ambushes most often occur near bends in the river. At bends, the control of the craft is more difficult and the river channel generally runs closer to one shore than the other, forcing the craft out of the middle of the waterway, toward the shore, and within range of the hidden ambushers.

While riverine ambushes can be extremely simple, they are often much more complex. Riverine ambushes are often multiple pointed. A series of ambushes may be mounted from the shore using rockets, command- or contact-detonated explosives, and automatic weapons. Typically, the boat will attempt to speed from the kill zone, only to move into another ambush.

Defensive Measures

The key points in defending against an ambush in restricted waters are as follows:

❏ Get people under cover.
❏ Call for assistance.
❏ Maneuver out of the area at maximum safe speed.
❏ Fire red distress flares, initiate Grimes lights and strobes, and set off the ship's horn so that other craft in the area know you are in distress.
❏ Illuminate their craft and yours with spotlights or flares to attract attention to your dilemma.
❏ Return fire if weapons are available.

Of course, the best way to avoid narrow waterway attacks is to avoid all areas where they may occur. If you must go into a danger area, plan your course track carefully along the narrow passage. Utilize busy routes where there is a large amount of traffic. Plan to sail when traffic is heaviest. Being alone and sailing in uninhabited waterways attracts specific attention to your vessel.

THE PROBLEM AHEAD

"Everything old is new again" is more than just a saying. Whether by chance or design, maritime terrorism is slowly moving to a new old paradigm: the armed vessel of commerce that raids commercial supply lines and destroys its targets in support of a cause rather than capturing vessels for personal exploitation or ransom.

Traditionally, navies are designed to protect the commercial fleets of their own country and escort friendly vessels. Warship-to-warship engagements are designed to knock out the opponent's navy and deny the opponent the ability to escort and protect its commercial fleet. When the main battle fleet of an enemy is decimated and can no longer protect its merchant vessels, the victor's naval arm can attack the enemy's commercial fleet at will, destroy commerce, wreck an economy, and eventually force the surrender of the enemy.

A country or enemy with a deficient fleet, or no fleet at all, is forced to use subterfuge to remain competitive in sea warfare. Historically, the weapon of choice has been armed civilian vessels, disguised somehow, and used as raiders. These armed merchant cruisers can conduct decisive offensive warfare against supply lines and commercial channels.

The story of armed merchant cruisers goes back to the time of letters of marque. These government-issued letters authorized private operators to attack enemy shipping. When the European wars that spawned letters of marque ended, many of the militarized private ships turned pirate, starting what some said was the great age of piracy.

In the U.S. Civil War, armed merchant cruisers served as the southern navy in place of purpose-built warships.

In World War I, Germany used armed merchant cruisers to great effect. Surface raiders severed supply lines and communications between the Allies and Russia at a key time when the Russians needed the materials. The supply deprivation helped lead to the massive Russian losses suffered by the czar's troops and may well have been a significant factor in bringing about the Russian Revolution.

When the German Navy was reduced to a virtual coast guard after World War I, German rearmament began in 1927 with planning for a fleet of four armed merchant cruisers. The German strategy was based on the fact that the German navy, and allied nations that became known as the Axis, essentially had no overseas bases from which the ships could operate. To create a worldwide maritime threat—a threat that had to be countered by the Allied navies—the armed merchant cruisers would have to go to sea, remain operational for months that sometimes turned into years, and utilize supply vessels in place of land bases.

As small as the German raider force in World War II was—ultimately only nine vessels—the Allied navies had to expend stupendous efforts to counter it. The convoy system was instituted on main trading routes to protect shipping against U-boats and raiders, but at a tremendous cost in time and fuel. The economies of individual shipping— quick turnaround, speedy delivery of goods—were sacrificed to the need to keep ships in harbor while assembling the convoy and limiting the speed of the convoy to the slowest vessel. When ships could not be assembled into convoys, warships had to be assigned to patrol key areas where shipping passed through, or shipping suffered lengthy diversions to avoid areas where raiders were believed to operate. Detours were expensive in time and fuel. The transport of food and war materials suffered.

During World War II, the raiders accomplished the goal that the German Admiralty sent them out to do. Between 1940 and 1943, the nine armed merchant cruisers—freighters converted with heavy weapons—sank more than 130 vessels, over 850,000 tons of shipping. Operating in Atlantic, Pacific, Arctic, Antarctic, and Indian waters, the cruisers exacted a toll that equaled that of German mines and was three

German armed merchant cruiser *Atlantis* in the South Atlantic, April 1941. (ww2db.com)

times the tonnage that German warships were able to sink. It took Allied forces about three and a half years to eliminate the menace of these nine ships. During that time, the Allies diverted military assets that could have been used against the U-boat threat or for fighting the war in Europe and Asia. The menace of the raiders forced merchant vessels to travel in slow-moving convoys, which tied up many war vessels and slowed the vital supply chain. The need for extra personnel everywhere drained the pool of trained manpower

Studying the results of the German armed merchant cruiser war, some things can be learned:

- Armed merchant cruisers can exact a heavy toll on shipping and world trade.
- They can spread navies thin.
- Vessels sailing alone, or with an inadequate escort, are particularly at risk.

- Hunting groups—teams of ships and aircraft—appear to be the most effective counter to merchant cruiser depredations.
- Fuel economy of the raider is important.
- Heavy weapons to incapacitate or sink a target vessel at the moment of attack are essential.
- Attacks must be made quickly, before the target vessel can get off a distress signal.

How does this relate to maritime terrorism today? Al-Qaeda's announced overall strategy is to damage and eventually destroy the economic capabilities of the West. The evidence of its attacks and other key tactical events support that strategy. Transportation lines and commerce—whether in the air, over water, or across land—are targeted. Al-Qaeda's leadership understands supply lines, just-in-time deliveries, and important choke points of commerce.

Whether the late Osama bin Laden actually owned or controlled the 10 merchant vessels that some intelligence agencies said he did in 2001 may not be important; ships can always be procured for a price. His surviving cohorts have shown an understanding of maritime tactics, attacking both warships and commercial vessels with suicide craft. Those manpower-light attacks have had limited success, damaging their targets to varying degrees but not sinking the targeted vessels.

There are tenuous indications that at least part of the multimillion dollar ransoms for ships and crews off the coast of Africa may be going to support the al-Qaeda war effort. Should Al-Qaeda be able to use these funds to obtain the correct kinds of ships from the maritime pool, crew those vessels with sailors dedicated to the cause, and get the required offensive weapons on the gray or black markets, the West could face the same type of problems the Allies did in World War II.

New surface raiders could easily disguise their offensive weaponry as deck cargo, just as the German raiders did. Unlike the situation in World War II, where raiders had to close within a few thousand feet of their target, giving an early indication of their possible nefarious intention, a modern raider armed with such antishipping missiles as the

French Exocet or Chinese Silkworm could easily stand off on the horizon as a passing ship and deliver a one-two punch that would sink a passing vessel before it had time to get off a radio message that it was under attack. The last part is key, since during World War II, radio messages from vessels that were under attack, or were being approached by a raider, helped identify the location of the attacker.

The evolution of terrorist naval warfare to the use of armed merchant cruisers is debatable, but the evidence suggests there is movement in that direction.

MARITIME DEFENSE

BEATING THEM AT THEIR OWN GAME

Pirates and maritime terrorists always hold the high cards. Theirs is the choice of the hunter, the choice of time and place, the advantage of knowing that every ship is a potential quarry. The navies of the world labor under a major disadvantage, on the other hand, for the quarry they seek is just one of the fleet, and every ship they encounter has to be treated as a potential enemy. Therefore, any commercial vessel or pleasure craft sailing into troubled waters must be prepared to fend for itself rather than expect an overburdened naval or coast guard unit to respond.

The ship operator or yacht owner has a simple operational sequence to follow:

- Detect
- Deter
- Destroy

Before engaging that operational sequence, the captain and crew of any high-value vessel—particularly one carrying material or people having ransom potential—have to be prepared and properly trained. And that begins before the vessel sets out.

PREPARING FOR TROUBLE

Vigilance is the key to self-protection, and it starts onboard. Your vessel's security personnel need to know every member of the crew, and if guests or passengers are expected, the security people need to know the details regarding those passengers and guests. Such information as their time and means of arrival and nature of their business is vital. Every crewmember also has a duty to be aware of—and on the lookout for—suspicious craft or people and then report the information appropriately. A pirate or terrorist can be anybody or any vessel.

Security Officer

The above paragraph implies that your vessel will have designated security responsibilities to one or more individuals. The responsibility of those duties should go to an individual who is mature, understanding of the threat, knows the vessel's strengths and weaknesses, and is willing—and has the dedicated time—to make the vessel safer in all regards from a security perspective.

Merchant ships are required to have a designated security officer who has been schooled in Safety of Life at Sea (SOLAS) and International Ship and Port Facility Security (ISPS) Code requirements and up-to-date pubs. Due to crew size of a typical ship, the security officer status would likely be collateral duty. Regardless, the security officer is still required to establish a ship's security plan (SSP)

Before going into an area of political unrest or where there are other known potential risks, the security chief researches the threat level. Where the risk is substantial, it is important to ask if the trip is really necessary and consider the possible tradeoffs of putting the vessel and crew in harm's way.

Security Assessment

Prior to sailing, the owner or operator of any valuable vessel should have a security assessment done on the vessel and crew. This should include an assessment of the proposed sailing plan as well as a study identifying the capabilities of the vessel, equipment, and crew with regard to dealing with maritime bandits. It should point out both strengths and weaknesses and provide recommendations for improving vessel capabilities and training of the crew. It should include recommendations regarding the need for professionals to either train the crew on contingencies or augment the crew, providing enhanced protection during the cruise. Even if the crew is not augmented by professional security personnel, the assessment provides a valuable awareness of the limitations and weaknesses of the vessel and crew.

Presail Briefing

Prior to getting underway, the captain of any vessel sailing in potentially hostile waters should get all hands together for a presail meeting. The agenda should include the following:

- ❏ Purpose of sailing.
- ❏ The vessel's itinerary, including length of time.
- ❏ Ports of call.
- ❏ Standard operating procedures for crew and guests/passengers aboard.
- ❏ Navigational briefing (including tracks, time lines, and filing a sailing plan).
- ❏ Communication briefing of who to contact in an emergency, schedule for radio checks, and other commo planning.
- ❏ Intelligence briefing of the area (geopolitical, cultural, etc.).
- ❏ Threat briefing regarding the pirates or terrorists of the region.
- ❏ Attack philosophy—the tactics and techniques common to pirates or terrorists in these waters.
- ❏ Defense philosophy—the tactics and techniques to be used in defensive situations.
- ❏ The role to be played by each individual in an emergency.
- ❏ Any changes to the plan once underway.
- ❏ Port visitation policies and security measures.

DETECT

The key to thwarting pirates or maritime terrorists is to detect any possible attack before seagoing ruffians can get alongside the hull, and certainly before they can get aboard. The boat's deck is a dividing line of sorts. For that reason, vessels with a low freeboard, where attackers can quickly gain the deck, are especially vulnerable. When boarders are still trying to get on deck, you, as the defender, have the advantage. When the attackers gain the deck, the odds will shift. Even though the advantage is not always in favor of the attacker at that point, it is still true that those on the vessel have lost much of their previous advantage. This is particularly true if the attackers are armed.

No matter where you are, in safe harbor or dangerous waters, it is essential to always be observant and continually sharpen the crew's powers of observation. Only after the threat has been detected can

This ship has done all the right countermeasures—water hoses, barbed wire, warning signs, even dummy watchstanders—and it still got hijacked by pirates and had to be rescued by the U.S. Navy. In the world of piracy, nothing is 100-percent foolproof. (U.S. Navy photo)

maritime attackers be deterred. Detection requires a mix of good watch procedures, competent personnel, and adequate equipment.

Watch

Watchstanders have to move around the ship, checking over the side often, particularly in those areas where boarders would be most likely to put their boat or raft while they sneak aboard. Pirates' favorite weak spots include the stern and anywhere the ship's bulk overhangs the water. The ship's boarding ladder should be well-secured—and locked into place if possible—so that boarders cannot simply snip the cable and have the stairway rumble down to greet them.

In the case of open ocean steaming, radar is one of the most important devices next to a good set of Mark 1, Mod 0 eyeballs. A good lookout at the radar station, or looking 180 degrees astern, is second.

Lookouts on merchant ships operating anywhere near Somalia should pay special attention to indigenous craft carrying or towing a number of small boats. The small skiffs traditionally used by Somali pirates do not have the range for operations hundreds of miles from the coast. Nowadays they are using longer-range indigenous craft as mother ships to give them both the cover and the striking range well beyond what they once enjoyed. These pirates continue to move their operations not only further out into the Indian Ocean but further south along the East African coastline. This makes it tougher for naval forces to patrol a vastly increased territory, which is exactly what they hoped to achieve.

The mother ship can be anything from a native dhow to a captured tug. Sometimes the pirates will press the crew of a captured vessel into service. Once the pirate crew has spotted a target, they will get the mother ship within range, but not close, and launch her skiffs. The skiffs are the armed attack boats that will dash out and try to board. If the watchstanders report skiffs launching from an indigenous vessel, institute full defensive actions immediately.

It is important to remember that terrain masking and camouflage may be used to hide pirates or other ambushers. They can lurk in a

This dhow is a pirate mother ship. The giveaway is the two white skiffs in tow. Once a target is spotted, the mother ship gets within launch range for skiffs. The skiffs then make a high-speed dash to the target vessel. (U.S. Navy photo)

cove, hidden against the backdrop of the land, until a potential victim passes close beside. Then they may come pelting out. It is important to watch the water's edge of nearby land formations for any movement when transiting pirate-prone waters.

Detection Equipment

No specific piece of equipment can be a panacea in detecting approaching trouble. Therefore, all available resources have to be used simultaneously, creating an effective, interlocking detection system.

A radar system that is well tuned to detect small and large craft alike is among the most effective tools. It can warn of the approach of dangerous craft in time to launch an effective defense against the intruders. Radar should be used for this purpose while underway at sea, when anchored, or when moored in port. Crewmembers also need to understand the limitations of radar. (See "The Limits of Radar" below.)

A vessel's detection equipment should include a lighting system that allows for constant illumination of the water around an anchored craft. In addition, ships should have spotlights that can cover 360 degrees.

Vision-enhancing equipment such as good binoculars, night-vision devices (NVDs), and intrusion-detection devices (IDDs) should be available to all watchstanders in pirate- or terrorist-prone areas. The ability of NVDs to detect a small craft—or any object—depends on the amount of ambient light available. By rule of thumb, under a half moon a small craft may be detectable at a half mile or more.

Sonar offers less of a chance of detecting threats under normal circumstances but can still be effective in certain instances. Sonar may detect the noise of an approaching vessel engine, and in rare instances it has proven effective in detecting approaching small submersibles or divers. (Divers or submarines may be used to destroy or damage the vessel or to plant drugs at one port that can then be removed at the next port. The sophistication of drug runners, pirates, or other seagoing criminals cannot be underestimated.)

Again, the most important vision aid is the Mark 1 Mod 0 human eyeball, which is very effective in detecting approaching problems before they get too close. Alertness of the individual is the key here. Vigilance should be at a heightened state in areas known for piracy or terrorism.

Reducing Your Own Detectability

If pirates can't detect you, they cannot board you, so commercial captains and yacht owners traveling in piracy-prone areas may want to consider ways of reducing their own detectability.

Expect pirates to have some sophistication. They are experienced and battle-hardened seamen who have improved their techniques through the years since the black flag flew over the Spanish Main. Expect that they will have aboard at least field glasses, night-vision devices, and radar.

In troubled waters, the best technique for any vessel is to stay well out to sea, avoiding the coastline and staying out of striking range of small craft (understanding that mother ships can still transport pirates far out). Planned sailing tracks, based on good intelligence, can greatly assist in avoiding confrontations at sea.

Visual spotting depends upon sea state, sky condition, clarity of the horizon, and time of day. The color of the hull and masts, if they do not blend in with the background, may well be a detriment. Many parts on a boat will reflect light like a mirror, pinpointing your location to people who might otherwise miss your craft completely. Anyone can get crazy about things like this. Windscreens, for instance, have high reflectability. So does chrome. So who is going to take out the windows or paint the fittings flat black?

How serious a detriment these items are to safety is really an open question. Even cherry-red masts would not be a problem unless and until you run into a pirate. Choosing a color scheme and reducing reflectivity to reduce detectability is not a bad idea for yacht owners—many of the pirates do it—but whether this would really prove worthwhile is more a matter of the owner's point of view than any other consideration. Commercial vessels restricted to their house colors may not have the option to alter their color scheme.

Visual detectability actually depends upon more than just detection of the vessel itself. The wake is highly detectable. This is becoming more of a factor because of modern technology. Thermal-imaging devices are available that can detect even minute differences in temperature, such as found in wakes where the water after a moving boat is in fact quite different in temperature from the surrounding sea.

Even without thermal-detection devices, a pirate can use the wake and spray generated by a vessel as a principal visual indicator. As a rule of thumb, sea state 3 and speeds of less than 2 knots will normally eliminate wake as a means of detection. Under such conditions, the waves create enough surface disruption to mask it.

Disguising the wake may be a more important factor for the successful pirate than it is to the potential victim. No vessel owner or captain is going to dog-paddle his craft around the seven seas in sea state 3 and above just to eliminate the possibility of wake detection.

The high visibility of a wake, on the other hand, works *against* the pirate or terrorist attempting to attack an anchored vessel. Because of wake visibility, any would-be attackers may have to rely on tidal flow and current to quietly drift their boat into proper position. Instead of motors, they may use paddles or poles to propel an ambush craft. But all those things take time—and the extra time gives the defender more time to spot the intruder and prepare for action. That is why alert, all-around watches while at anchor are so important.

Bioluminescence, or the production of light by minute marine life such as certain types of plankton, is another means of visual detection. The bioluminescent scar is generally most visible on dark nights with high cloud cover and low sea state. Higher sea states and a bright moon or stars reflecting off the ocean surface virtually eliminate any chance for a hostile party to use bioluminescence to detect your vessel's path.

The Limits of Radar

Most ships rely heavily on radar to detect potential pirates. Captains and crew monitor the radar for unidentified blips—especially ones that are moving fast or are on an intercept course. (Anything moving on an intercept course should be treated as if it were carrying a boarding party.) But the fact is that radar is only marginally capable of detecting the type of small craft many pirates use. The captain of a ship has to wring the most out of his set. Tuning and reading the radar, then, becomes all important.

Every radar has its blind spots, and those dead zones vary not only with the radar but with the weather conditions and sea state. One blind spot of most radar is just behind the antenna, the result of mounting the antenna on the forward part of the mast where it is most effective for navigating the ship. This blind spot is well known and often used by attackers.

It is important to test the vessel's radar against a target craft to see where the weak spots occur in coverage and to plug those holes. If detection capability tests have not been carried out, assume that the radar cannot pick up a blip from a small craft within 500 yards of the vessel or beyond 7,000 yards. As noted above, an area of reduced/denied detection is often directly to the stern of the ship in the 170- to 180-degree relative region. For that reason, stern watches are critical, whether the vessel is anchored or in transit.

When possible, pirates may choose periods of higher sea state (3 or above) to minimize the probability of detection. Not only is it more difficult to visually spot the approach of a small craft under these conditions, the already degraded radar operation is further exploited by reducing the approach speed to mask signatures in the sea clutter. For pirates, the general rule is the less wake the better when approaching a target vessel.

While pirates generally prefer bow-on penetration, since it usually minimizes radar cross section, the fact is that when small craft operate in a zigzag pattern, they are often more difficult to detect and track. This is due to the inability of radar operators to establish a constant track from which to project target location.

Small craft traveling parallel to the direction of the swell are generally more detectable by radar than those running perpendicular to it. Marauders know it—through the fraternity of thugs and from individual experience—and are likely to make use of that fact.

Small pirate vessels can avoid radar detection by operating at or near channel markers or other large buoys. The radar's return off the pirate vessel will often be confused with, or masked by, the return off the buoy. Radar does not do a good job of discriminating between a buoy and a small craft in close proximity, nor will it determine that small craft are located at a buoy. This is another reason an alert lookout watch must be stood.

DETER

A watch, quarter, and station bill should be made out to repel boarders, whether underway or in port. The crew must prepare by employing some or all of the following measures:

❑ Make certain that boarding gangways are locked in their "up" position at night or during any period of reduced visibility.

❑ Where technically possible, ensure boarding ladders are locked into place or braced so that simply snipping a cable will not release them.

❑ Ensure that anchor cables or other lines extending from the ship do not facilitate surreptitious boarding. Cones and razor wire can effectively close these areas as entry points.

❑ Make it difficult for a craft of any size, or even swimmers, to approach the anchored vessel without being spotted.

❑ Secure access hatches and portals to the interior.

❑ Secure tools (e.g., fire axes, nonessential ladders) topside that would allow boarders to gain access to the interior of the ship.

❑ Try to have only one access way to the bridge, and lock all entry/exit ways to the bridge. Where possible, remove outside ladders from lower decks to the bridge.

❑ Move all personnel into a preplanned "safe room" (described in more detail below).

❑ When sailing the Gulf of Aden and Somali pirate waters, sandbag the bridge and the aft lookout position to protect crew from small arms fire.

Essential defensive equipment may include:

❑ Radar in good working order, optimally tuned for the conditions, and constantly monitored even at anchor to spot approaching small vessels.

❑ Satellite tracking system to communicate the ship's position at all times to maritime security authorities.

❑ Flares, sirens, searchlights, and strobe lights to attract attention to the attempts of the attackers.

❑ Deck-level fencing, topped by barbed or razor wire, to deter boarding. The fence or razor wire may be electrified.

❑ Fire hoses for repelling boarders.

Ships at anchor and in port can get careless and leave gangways down, allowing easy access to unauthorized personnel from other ships. This is especially true if crews become complacent about watch duties. (Jim Gray photo)

❏ Foam-dispensing equipment to make the deck slippery if attackers are able to board.

❏ Netting attached to the sides and stern of the ship to drag in the water in order to foul propulsion systems of approaching small craft.

❏ Camera surveillance systems, covering at least the most likely or most vulnerable boarding spots.

❏ Acoustic deterrence devices.

❏ Small handheld radios, which have an important role in all inter-vessel communications but become particularly important during antipiracy actions.

❏ Compressed-air horns for instantaneous alerting of everyone aboard the craft—passengers and crew—in case of trouble.

❏ Polymer coating on the glass of the bridge's inside portholes to provide a degree of protection from small arms fire, shrapnel, and flying glass. It is an aftermarket add-on and is reasonably priced.

One of the greatest deterrents to pirates is their loss of the element of surprise. If they know they have been spotted—particularly if they are aware that countermeasures are being taken even before they have made an effective and aggressive move—many will back off and wait for some less-observant crew to come along. Demonstrating that the crew and vessel are prepared and alert is a key element of deterrence. The exception to this appears to be the tactics of Somali pirates in that they often come alongside and simply begin shooting RPGs and small arms at the targeted vessel, often while their brethren come up from astern and attempt to climb onto the deck.

Using the Launch

In harbor or at anchor, one of the greatest assets to deterring piracy is the proper use of the launch that moves crew and guests ashore and back. Once any approaching craft enters a self-described perimeter security zone, the launch can and should be used to intercept it.

When used as a floating interceptor, the launch deters the curious and the dangerous from approaching the vessel. Moreover, the use of a standoff launch sends a message that the crew is alert and will not be a willing target of opportunity, prompting most would-be attackers to go elsewhere in search of victims. The launch is not a means of stopping pirates; it is an early-warning device. An approaching craft that evades or ignores the launch must be considered a threat.

Generally, the launch should have a native speaker aboard, if possible. The craft leaves the mother ship and approaches an incoming vessel, requesting that it lay off and depart the area of the larger vessel for security reasons. The launch crew should report anything suspicious noted during its approach to the intruding vessel.

The launch can also be used when alongside a pier to check under and around the pier and to conduct antiswimmer operations. The launch can approach an unfamiliar pier, check for security, and guide the vessel to the best pierside approach. It can also assist in line handling for the vessel.

Effective launch operations require the following:

❑ Good communications between the vessel and launch and any other links in the system.

❑ A powerful spotlight or flashlight that is fully charged or supplied with fresh batteries.

❑ A loudspeaker system.

❑ Flashing lights or similar strobe or lighting systems.

❑ A native speaker or someone familiar with the appropriate phrases.

❑ Shotgun or other appropriate weapons systems where legally permitted.

❑ A qualified crew of two individuals at a minimum.

Other Deterrence Measures

If a craft's path converges with your vessel and you are suspicious, increase your speed and attempt to exit the area. Assume the converging vessel is a threat. Reverse course if necessary to avoid contact with incoming vessels. When vessels maneuver in an attempt to block your ship, zigzag through at flank speed. Ramming the other vessel is always a possible danger and in fact may be required.

If attackers should succeed in coming alongside an anchored vessel, the watch can twist the vessel in place by running engines at the highest RPM possible. This makes it extremely difficult for attackers to come aboard, especially if they employ many boats. Where the situation demands and attackers pose an immediate threat to the life of the crew, open containers of flammable liquids can be tossed into attacking boats and set alight with flares.

At anchor or in port, the engineering department and deck crew can help deter attack by swimmers. Randomly turning the sea suction intakes on and off, or turning the screws, keeps most swimmers at a distance. Occasionally, dropping M-80 firecrackers with weights over the sides and dangling grappling hooks, or even the largest-size fishing hooks, over the sides can also deter approaching swimmers.

On low-freeboard vessels, whether anchored or at sea, a wall of chain-link fencing running the entire length of the vessel—8 to 10 feet high—makes boarding more difficult. If the fencing—which allows the crew unobstructed visibility—can be angled, outboard attackers will have a significantly more difficult time boarding. This is particularly true when fire hoses are available to swat the boarders off as they try to scale the fencing. The fencing can be laced with razor wire or barbed wire to add another level of antiboarding protection.

DESTROY

Destroy is the last resort for the mariner, but it is not the end game move. Pleasure boaters or merchant seamen should not have to do the work of coast guards or the military. The ideal is always to detect any attack in good time, escape from the pirates or terrorists, and exit the area. Notify local or international authorities and provide all observations to them. That is the best outcome.

But if attackers are detected and even then refuse to be deterred, they may be destroyed in self-defense. Effective means of resistance should be available to the crew—just in case events come down to that.

In something as complex as counterboarding operations, it is unwise to leave the crew reactions to instinct, snap judgments, or even dumb luck. The captain and crew must train as a team, and they must work as a team. There must be a defense plan, and the crew must be versed in that plan. But a crew also needs the tools to deter armed attackers.

Usually a captain and crew should be armed with weapons that would allow them to resist anything smaller than a naval gunboat.

The crew must have experience with any weaponry kept onboard, and they must have conducted drills with it for all contingencies. Planning, and then exercising the knowledge, pays instant bonuses if the vessel faces pirates or maritime thugs of any kind.

Firearms

The history of maritime law has long allowed American vessels, including merchantmen, to be armed to defend themselves against pirates and maritime criminals. In colonial times, merchant ships carried the same type of armaments—including cannon—that were found on naval craft.

In the early 20th century, the United States recognized that merchant vessels could carry guns similar to those on naval vessels, so long as they were relatively few in number and within certain size limits. Small arms were also allowed, provided they and the ammunition stocks were not excessive. Vessels had to follow normal trade routes and be manned by civilian crews to maintain their merchant navy status. To be eligible, the vessels had to avoid carrying contraband as well.

U.S. law codified maritime self-defense with 33 USCS § 383, "Resistance of pirates by merchant vessels." Under that law, the captain and crew of any U.S. merchant vessel—one owned wholly, or in part, by a U.S. citizen—may oppose and defend against any aggression, search, restraint, depredation, or seizure, and may subdue and capture the attacker(s) and send the pirates to any U.S. port.

International law also allows crews of merchantmen to carry and use arms for self-defense. The 1982 United Nations Convention on the Law of the Sea, known as UNCLOS, says that all states and the vessels that fly their flags enjoy the freedom of navigation in Exclusive Economic Zones (EEZs) and on the high seas. Within territorial seas up to 12 nautical miles from the coastal baseline, ships enjoy the right of innocent passage. If pirates attempt to deprive ships of their right to freedom of navigation, the ship owner and vessel's crew may take reasonable steps to defend the vessel and its personnel. Those defensive steps, written into the vessel security plan, may involve everything from deterrence measures like razor wire and armor to the use of firearms.

Self-defense measures involving firearms must always be proportionate to the threat. Firing warning shots at a threatening vessel does not constitute the use of force. A failure to heed warning shots or other oral warnings generally justifies shooting at the attacker's rudder or propeller area/outboard engine. Shooting to kill is justified only when a vessel comes under hostile fire itself or is in imminent danger of illegal boarding and seizure.

Local Rules

Under maritime law, the country that flags a vessel may set the rules on the use of weapons by the crews of merchant vessels. But all such regulations must comply with the laws and contingencies of the sovereign nations through whose waters the ship will pass. Knowing the law, and obeying it, will save many problems.

Within territorial waters, the crew of a merchantman should not conduct weapons practice or do anything that could be construed as a threat or use of force against the sovereignty, territorial integrity, or political independence of the controlling state.

Generally, governments of ports of call may restrict the possession and use of weapons by crews of ships flying a foreign flag while those vessels are in port. As a rule, the presence of weapons should be specifically provided for in the vessel's security plan, which must be approved by the government whose flag the ship is flying. When in port, or entering or leaving territorial waters during a port call, all firearms should be unloaded and locked below deck under the supervision of the captain.

That situation may pose problems in ports where security is problematic. In ports where criminal activity and piracy are a known perennial problem, the safest practical measure may be to lock up the vessel's weapons and hire local security personnel for on-board protection after discussing the situation with reliable port authorities.

For American ships, weapons and sufficient ammunition supplies should always be brought aboard and locked up while the vessel is in a U.S. port and *before* it sails to foreign ports. Many boat owners have found how extremely difficult it can be to bring weapons aboard a U.S. vessel legally while docked in a foreign port. Most countries have restrictions on the possession of firearms, or at least their possession by noncitizens. Trying to bring guns aboard the vessel at locations outside the United States can range from difficult to impossible.

If a vessel's owner decides on arming crewmembers, the crew will require training in both pirate tactics and the safe, legal use of weaponry. Hiring armed guards or vessel protection detachments (VPDs; see below) may eliminate part of that training, but the use of VPDs requires careful study of both the company providing the guards and the qualifications of the personnel to be assigned to the ship. Armed guards who have little or no experience in working with merchant vessels and crewmembers may be a liability. The preferred choice is to use former professional military personnel with a background in vessel protection and ship boarding and who make it their business to know the law regarding use of deadly force on the high seas and in port.

The Shipboard Arsenal

No single weapon will work best in all cases of need. A combination of firearms is needed for the weaponry suite on commercial vessels, yachts, and other ships. The well-stocked ship's arsenal should include handguns, rifles, and shotguns.

The first point to understand is that a firearm is only as good as its shooter. Using weapons in real life is not something from a Hollywood movie. Hitting a target with any firearm is difficult at any time, but accuracy is particularly elusive when the shooter is on a rocking, rolling deck on the high seas and the target is firing back. That is part of the reason why the presence of a well-trained VPD is generally preferable to weapons-trained crewmembers.

Handguns can be a suitable choice for watchstanders, particularly

The *Maersk Alabama*. This famous ship was boarded in 2009 and its hostage captain saved by U.S. Navy SEAL snipers during ransom negotiations. The *Maersk Alabama* has been attacked by Somali pirates twice since 2009. Each time, the pirates were repelled by vessel protection detachments on board. (U.S. Navy photo)

in ports where that is permitted. They are easy to access and, unlike larger weapons, are easy to carry around the vessel. However, unless the shooter is a well-trained marksman, a handgun is often ineffective as a defensive weapon to keep intruders off the ship.

Handguns usually come into their own when used for self-defense after attackers have already penetrated the vessel. By contrast, a rifle—particularly a semiautomatic 7.62mm rifle—is effective in repelling boarders or intruders before they gain the deck. In the hands of a trained marksman, the rifle, with its fair range and good penetration, can be quite effective. Witness the shooting performed by U.S. Navy SEALs in subduing the pirates who hijacked the *Maersk Alabama* in 2009.

But the single best all-around weapon for defense of a vessel is a stainless steel 12-gauge shotgun—the stainless part being essential to minimize the corrosive effects of the maritime environment on the weapon.

Handguns are too inaccurate for even close-quarter battle at sea, except in the hands of expert marksmen. Rifles may be useful in trying to keep attackers at some distance from the vessel, but again, they tend to be inaccurate when fired from a heaving, rolling ship. Shotguns, however, provide good target acquisition up to at least 25 meters. The shot pattern gives a wide area of coverage. When rifled slugs are available, the shotgun can be used effectively against the wheelhouse, engine spaces, and even the hull of many attacking craft.

The vessel should carry a supply of various types of shotgun ammunition—including rifled slugs—but the standard load for the weapon is generally #4 or 00 buck. Plan to bring enough ammunition to permit frequent and substantial training and practice.

Each vessel owner and captain has to establish a standard operating policy for the use and storage of firearms, and it should be written into the ship's plan for defense. Factors to consider include:

❏ What weapons will be aboard?
❏ Who will be trained to use them?
❏ Who will be authorized to use them?
❏ Where will they be placed for easy access both at sea and in port?
❏ Will they be kept locked in their locations(s)?
❏ Where is each weapon post onboard?
❏ When will they be kept at the ready?
❏ Under what circumstances will they be used?
❏ How will the countries visited regulate their existence?

Other Weaponry

Whether or not guns of any type will be carried aboard a vessel, the ship should have a stock of nonlethal weaponry.

Nonlethal standoff weapons for use against boarders include high-pressure fire hoses, flare guns, sound machines, and blinding lights directed at the eyes of attackers. When obtainable, flash-bang grenades and riot tear gas guns can be used effectively to deter and confuse boarders. Electronic stun guns of at least 120,000 volts of power and OC-10 pepper gas may be effective at close range, but if pirates are close enough for these to be useful, resistance has become a hand-to-hand affair and is probably a lost cause. (Don't forget to take the wind direction into account when using tear gas or sprays.)

Molotov cocktails—any of the improved kind that do not require an open flame but use flares or chemicals for ignition—may be dropped on pirate craft that have come alongside a vessel. Smoke floats are another possibility to confuse the perpetrators with regard to the location and approach of their vessel against yours.

DEFENSE STRATEGY AGAINST
THE TWO BASIC ATTACK PROFILES

There are really only two basic strategies of aggression: urgent and deliberate attacks.

An urgent attack is most often associated with a military patrol boat or a heavily armed pirate craft that believes it is far better armed and faster than its prey. Terrorists conducting a suicide attack would also be likely to adopt this method. In the urgent attack, the vessel closes on the commercial vessel or yacht at high speed, along a straight course. It makes little use of cover, concealment, or deception. The high-speed inbound contact—usually from radar, vision, or sometimes sound—gives target ships a good indication that the contact has potentially hostile intent.

Any high-speed inbound radar target, or one converging on your course, is highly suspect. Watching the vessel can giver further indications of hostility. Key indicators include the following:

❏ A weapons mount (or covered area that could house a heavy weapon) in the bow.
❏ Visible arms in the craft.
❏ Disguises or masking of the crew's faces.
❏ An exceptionally large crew for the size of the craft.

❏ Motors larger than would normally be found on that type of craft.

When faced with an urgent attack style, the best move is to run, call for assistance, and immediately prepare to repel boarders or keep the attacker from striking your vessel in the case of a suicide attack.

The deliberate attack is often much more complex and convoluted. It is subject to an almost unlimited number of variations and permutations and may involve a number of pirate or terrorist craft.

A deliberate attack may involve prepositioning of the attack craft, in which case the attackers may not move at all. Instead, they carefully place their craft, or use ruses, so they do not have to make a long or obvious approach. Slow relative speeds used in prepositioning allow the attacking vessel to slowly close on the target ship in a nonthreatening manner. On the other hand, high-speed stern chases or bow approaches with lights blacked out in heavy weather, which masks detection, may also be used in the deliberate attack.

Cover and deception measures most commonly used in a deliberate attack include the following:

❏ Turning off all navigation lights and darkening the ship.
❏ Using zigzag approach courses.
❏ Employing deceptive lighting, such as fishing lights or dive lights.
❏ Rafting up with local fishing craft.
❏ Lying in ambush in a cove.
❏ Using merchant traffic for screening.
❏ Making judicious use of speed—either fast or slow.
❏ Employing ruses to encourage you to stop your vessel.

No matter which type of attack is used, whether the attack takes place in the open ocean or in a harbor, the target vessel usually must be boarded or surrendered. Pirates cannot achieve success unless they can seize control of the ship. For that reason, it makes sense to think of the hull and gunwales as castle walls. As long as they are not breached, as long as the raiders do not reach the deck, the defenders are in a relatively powerful position.

The Antipiracy Plan

Establishing an effective antipiracy plan (equally applicable to terrorist activity and other forms of hostile approach) requires the captain to draw up a watch, quarter, and station bill that takes piracy into account. Everyone is a lookout—no matter where they are.

The antipiracy plan involves drawing concentric circles around the ship. The first circle extends up to three miles out from the vessel. You want to be aware of anything or anyone within that circle; you need to observe all other vessels for suspicious activity. The radar watch, as well as visual identification, is important here. However, it is as important to avoid paranoia as it is to avoid complacency. There is no room on a ship for either. Since there are relatively few pirates in comparison with the number of boats throughout the world, there is generally little cause for alarm with regard to nearby craft. If they're more than a mile away, they have little ability to hurt you. Pirates have to get in closer. For those reasons, the first, and the best, clue to potential trouble is any boat moving closer to you.

At about a mile out, any craft (not just those traveling at high speed) that appears to be on an approaching or collision course should be considered a potential boarder. At that point, all available crew and even passengers should appear on deck—watching in the direction from which the perceived threat is coming. The more eyes the better. Pirates often rely on stealth and on the failure of the victim to see them until it is too late for effective action. The simple act of mustering passengers and crew along a rail, looking at the suspicious boat, will cause some pirates to give up the attack and seek a less alert, less troublesome target. This may not hold true with Somali pirates. They seem to relish simply shooting the target up with RPGs and small arms fire if they are unable to board surreptitiously, feeling it is in their best interest to frighten the target into stopping. But most piracy is nothing more than a seagoing ambush. If pirates can't take your vessel and those aboard by surprise, they

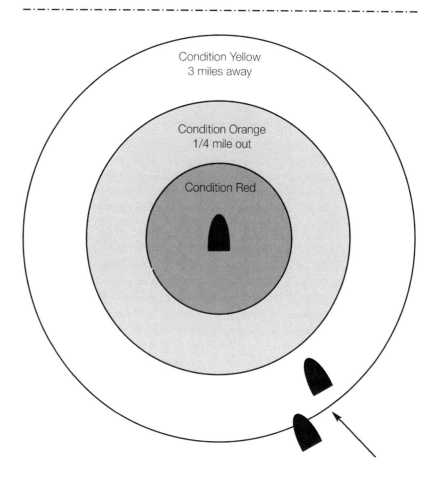

Condition Yellow
3 miles away

Condition Orange
1/4 mile out

Condition Red

MAINTAIN A 360° WATCH
There may be more than one
threat situation

Conditional alert stages for incoming threats.

are already in serious trouble. They know it. When you clearly demonstrate to them that they have been seen and are being watched carefully, they will often go elsewhere in search of less observant seafarers.

There is one caveat to putting all hands on deck to look at an approaching ship: make certain that the obvious approach is not being used to distract everyone so that a surprise attack can be mounted from another direction. In other words, maintain 360-degree security at all times. Keep an eye on the known intruder into your sea space, but at the same time be aware of any other vessels that may approach—or that you may be approaching unwittingly.

When the approaching vessel reaches the mile-out point, such nonlethal weaponry as fire hoses should be broken out and placed at strategic locations while designated crewmembers stand by to use them.

At a quarter mile, five minutes from potential contact (or when it is apparent that the approaching vessel is on a collision course), assigned crew should go into action stations. From here, take the following measures:

❏ Warn off the approaching vessel with lights, signal flags, voice communication, or radio.

❏ Designate at least one person to send an emergency radio transmission, making certain to give the location, the name of your vessel, and particulars about the suspicious vessel. While the message may not actually be transmitted yet, if your preparations and communications are monitored (and they may well be if the approaching craft is a pirate vessel), the intimations that a distress call is being prepared tend to end the matter right there.

❏ Order those aboard the ship who have been designated as noncombatants to leave the deck and go to a preplanned safety location in the vessel.

❏ Bring weapons to the deck and distribute to those people—crew and any passengers—assigned to repel the boarding party. The defenders should seek cover where possible and concealment where cover is not available.

Even if you have established radio communications with naval forces, you still risk being captured before they arrive on scene. (U.S. Navy photo)

❑ Start aggressive maneuvering of the vessel, making it difficult for unfriendly craft to come alongside. Fishtailing while traveling at the highest safe speed is often useful.

On the closer approach of any suspicious vessel—at approximately one minute from probably contact—fire a flare across the bow of the offending craft, followed by a rifle shot or shotgun blast. The distress call should now be made (it can always be retracted if necessary) if the intruder does not shear off or attempts to approach from a new angle. Contact by radio, a distress call, firing red flares in the air, illumination, and sounding distress horns should continue. Pirates do not want outside attention attracted to their illegal actions.

Close-Quarter Defensive Tactics
Maneuvering at all in close quarters requires some deftness. Most captains are taught to avoid collisions with another vessel at all costs. Yet when trying to fend off a boarding party, the smartest thing may well be to collide with the attacking craft. If it is smaller,

as most pirate vessels are, it may not stand up well in an encounter.

The attackers are expecting you to try to escape, and their plans have probably been based on the assumption that you will attempt to get away from them, not come closer to them. Depending on the height of your hull above the waterline, as well as the relative height of their deck, turning into them when you are on a parallel course, or across their intended course at close range, may disrupt the aim of any gunmen or knock potential boarders off their feet. Such a maneuver is almost guaranteed to cause a radical change of direction on their part unless they have no fears about the outcome of any collision.

Ramming is a subject few people want to talk about—rules of the road are part of the 10 commandments of seamanship and have been for millennia. But ramming an attacker is a viable defense.

The key to ramming a vessel is to strike a glancing blow. Do not attempt to run over the pirate vessel or cut the craft in half; the debris from the collision may damage your screws and struts, thereby decreasing your speed or halting your escape entirely.

Other defensive tactics at close quarters include the following:

❑ Execute a fishtail maneuver, i.e., go both fast and slow and make other irregular course changes. This makes boarding a severe hazard and may discourage the best pirate boat captain from coming alongside.

❑ Blind the pirate vessel's coxswain with a spotlight or with flares shot directly at him in nighttime attacks.

❑ Simultaneously employ all techniques and lethal/nonlethal weapons to stop the pirates from coming aboard.

Any signs of an attempted forcible boarding, such as the employment of grappling hooks or any gunfire from the intruder, should be considered active aggression. In that circumstance, defenders may fire at will and as their targets allow. A gunfight at sea is not the goal of antipiracy procedures, however, and should be considered the last resort or outcome. Nor is your purpose to capture any seagoing desperadoes and bring them to justice. That is a job for coast guards. Some Russians, after halting an attack by Somali pirates, apparently placed the marauders into a lifeboat and simply turned them loose and then sunk the pirates' boat on the high seas. This, however, was a legally questionable action taken by professional security force personnel. It should not be attempted by normal sailors.

In the event of an attempted forcible boarding, the goal for your craft and crew is simple: get out of there in one piece. Speeding away, maneuvering, and discouraging their boarding are the hallmarks of the battle after that point.

THE SAFE ROOM

If pirates get on board, the last resort is the "safe room" or "panic room," called the "citadel" by Europeans.

A safe room into which the crew can retreat if the ship is taken over allows military forces to storm the ship with minimum risk to the crew. Anyone outside the room is considered fair game. To be effective, safe rooms must be bulletproof and supplied with food, water, sanitation facilities, and communications equipment. Under ideal circumstances, the room would also have systems that could override the ship's engines and immobilize the vessel.

Considerations for Establishing a Safe Room

For a safe room to be effective, it should meet the following criteria:

❑ It must be able to hold the whole crew inside.
❑ It must be able to be locked from inside.
❑ It must have good airflow or air conditioning.
❑ There must be radios and extra batteries stored inside.
❑ Crew must be able to communicate with the outside world from the radios inside.
❑ It should be stocked with:
 ✓ food and water for crew for several days

On October 25, 2010, the German merchant ship *Beluga Fortune* was attacked by armed pirates in the Indian Ocean. The crew locked themselves in the vessel's safe room and sent out a distress call. The pirates abandoned the ship when they heard that the Royal Navy was on its way. Royal Marines from the *HMS Montrose* boarded the *Beluga Fortune* and released the uninjured crew from the safe room. (NATO ACO PAO photo)

✓ medical supplies
✓ toilet paper and buckets
✓ mattresses (Size of room will dictate how many can be used. Crew can rest in shifts.)
✓ copies of crew IDs
✓ personal cell phones

Safe rooms have been used again and again with success. On April 7, 2010, the German merchant vessel *Taipan* was captured by pirates. Because the ship's crew locked themselves in a safe room, Dutch Marines were able to perform an airborne raid, capturing 10 pirates and clearing the ship without fearing the crew would be caught in the crossfire. Safe rooms are now cited in best management practices of many shipping companies.

Safe rooms work best when used in conjunction with a layered defense. The first defensive zone, along the railings, is designed to keep pirates and maritime criminals from gaining the deck. But the defensive zones start—they don't end—there. In danger areas or areas of concern, the entire ship must be locked down, creating zone after zone that intruders must penetrate. The lock-down zones may be inside or outside the ship. Hatches, compartments, and passage-ways—not to mention the safe room—are closed off and locked.

In a typical case, if pirates are able to board, they have to struggle to get through locked doors to access the bridge. Even if they get on the bridge, they have to defeat each hatchway to move further along in the ship and look for the crewmembers, who have taken refuge in the safe room. That search costs the pirates the one commodity they do not have in the opening stages of a boarding—time. Seldom will pirates have the quantity and variety of tools needed to quickly defeat the locks on hatches and doors, and even when they get through one, they have to face another locked hatchway, another locked door. The time the boarders take in breaking down doors and hatches can allow rescuers, summoned through radios in the safe room, to arrive at the scene and apprehend the maritime criminals.

Procedures When Under Boarding Attack

1. Send distress signals of boarding via VHF channel 16, backup channel 8, and telcom with presiding maritime security organization in the area of operations (AO).
2. Set off emergency locating systems (e.g., ShipLoc, Inmarsat) and turn on AIS, which will continuously mark your position.
3. Shut down engines and all unnecessary systems and electronics and *drift*. Note: All crew must know where the emergency and auxiliary engines control panel is located and be able to shut down the engines.
4. Muster all crew in the safe room and lock it down, denying access to pirates. All crewmembers must be inside the room. If one

person is left outside, the concept is negated. The compartment should be set so it is locked from inside and there is no access from outside. The door, walls, deck, and ceiling should be strong enough that pirates cannot force entry or fire through them.

5. Once locked in, the captain and crew establish communications with naval rescue forces. With the ship's crew in the safe room, rescue forces can board and clear the pirates without fear of the crew being caught in crossfire. Currently, Somali pirates do not have the technical know-how to run a ship or even to sink a large ship fast before rescue forces can arrive on scene.

6. Those in the safe room must be prepared to WAIT for rescue.

7. Once the ship is cleared of pirates, the military will want the crew to exit the safe room and be accounted for. Crew must come out slowly, with hands visible and ID available. While it is a happy occasion to be freed, this is not the time for photography. The flash on a camera can make the military rescuers very nervous.

VESSEL PROTECTION DETACHMENTS

When skiffs dash out from the mother ship, the crew of the targeted vessel will not have much time to react to the rapidly closing threat. Because of the tactics used by these pirates, the presence of a vessel protection detachment (VPD) is recommended in high-risk transits. VPDs are trained to look for suspicious activity and respond to it, making them a desirable addition to the ship.

Most crewmembers have as their primary job the running of the ship and providing comfort to any guests aboard a yacht or commercial vessel. For other crewmembers, security is, at best, an additional duty that has a low priority. VPDs, however, have no other priority than assuring the safety of the ship and those aboard.

There is no single template for a VPD mission. It can be tailored to meet the requirements of all vessels, from merchant ship to megayacht. The watch depends on the area where the ship is sailing and the types and number of craft likely to be encountered, the defensive

A nest of fishing vessels in Malaysia anchored near a small island. A trained maritime security officer noticed the unusual electronic array on the second vessel from left—a possible clue of activities besides fishing. (Jim Gray photo)

and offensive capabilities of the vessel, and the likelihood of an attack at any given hour.

When integrated with a vessel's complement of guests, passengers, and crew, maritime-knowledgeable VPD professionals are not a burden to the crew but rather provide enhancement to the daily operations by performing such duties as watchstanding underway and in port, operating the vessel's small craft, assisting the owners and guests in SCUBA diving, handling of lines, underwater hull inspection and repair, and numerous other maritime disciplines.

Whether a vessel's VPD should have weapons is always an issue. In many countries and territorial waters, weapons—even those meant for defense—are banned. A VPD detachment can help navigate this tricky terrain and devise alternative defensive measures where necessary. VPD personnel can also provide professional training and teach awareness to the crew so that they, too, are prepared to act positively and instinctively in security situations even when they are not augmented by security personnel.

Owners, crew, and guests feel more comfortable and relaxed when they do not have to be concerned with vessel security during their voyages. Increased security opens new, exciting cruising areas where passengers and crew can experience the local adventure and ambiance without the fear of piracy, extortion, and pilferage.

Mariners don't leave port without lifeboats and survival equipment—though they hope and expect they will never need them. In some parts of the world, the risks of sailing need to be met with a "security lifeboat" provided by a VPD security contingent.

THE BOTTOM LINE

When confronted with a pirate attack, the captain has to make a decision whether to surrender, take flight, or fight. In almost all cases, the best thing—if the option is still open—is to flee while calling for assistance. Any decision to resist is much more complicated.

The decision to resist is based upon the expected chances of success and an appraisal of whether the attackers are likely to physically harm the crew and passengers even if no resistance is offered. The exception again is the Somali region, where once they have the vessel and crew, the cost of returning both of these assets may well be so high that the ransom can never be met.

If a member of the boarding party is killed, injured, or maimed in the process, and the pirates do succeed in taking over the boat, passengers or crew may be injured or killed in angry retaliation. In addition, there is a chance of incurring casualties among the boat's passengers or crew during the battle. But once gunfire has been exchanged, and particularly if the spirited defense has caused casualties among the pirates, there should be no consideration of ending the resistance.

It is probably too late to make the decision to resist once intruders are swarming over the taffrail. If they are already aboard by the time anyone notices them, the pirates have probably effectively taken over the ship. Few captains can organize an effective resistance in the few moments available between boarding and the seizure of the wheelhouse and/or engineering spaces.

Running away, although usually the best maneuver, is as fraught with problems as fighting. Keep in mind that those people aboard the intruder vessel probably know the maritime geography of the area intimately—or at least far better than you do if you are just transiting. For that reason, high-speed maneuvering in shoaling water is not recommended. On the open ocean there may be some advantage to ringing up flank speed and trying to escape simply by speed, particularly if the attack craft do not appear to be capable of keeping up with yours. But in coastal waters, the combination of high speed and a lack of attention to proper navigation can result in the loss of the ship. In fact, the pirates may be hoping you will go aground in your haste to flee. Running aground would put you at their mercy, since their vessels are usually more shallow-drafted. Then they could maneuver around and board your stranded vessel at will.

CHECKLISTS

ALERT STAGES

The following stages permit the vessel to set itself at certain conditions of readiness, depending upon the potential threat that it may be experiencing or the risk level of the area it may be transiting.

❑ Yellow Alert—Three-mile detection; focused radar and lookouts on contact and 360-degree watch.

❑ Orange Alert—Repel boarder stations. You have five minutes or less to man up these stations and have equipment ready.

❑ Red Alert—All antipiracy measures are being put into effect at the captain's call to keep craft from coming alongside.

Note: The watch, quarter, and station bill identifies all members of the crew, their particular assignment, and what role they play in each of the three stages of alert.

PRESAILING PREPARATION

Preparing a security plan before you sail is just good common sense. You don't get underway without fuel and provisions, so it stands to reason that a presailing checklist for hostile waters is in order. The following is an example of just some of the items to consider.

Detection Equipment
❏ Binoculars
❏ Radar
❏ Night-vision devices
❏ FLIR (forward-looking infrared)
❏ Intrusion-detection systems

Antiboarding Measures
❏ Firearms
❏ Physical systems
❏ Comm links with captain and defenders

Nonlethal Weapons
❏ LORAD (long-range active detection)
❏ Special nonlethal ammo:
  ✓ Bean bags
  ✓ Rubber bullets
  ✓ CS rounds
  ✓ Illumination
❏ Tasers
❏ Bear spray (for longer range)
❏ Pepper gas (for close range)
❏ Stun batons
❏ Standard batons
❏ Stun guns
❏ Fire hoses, charged

Route Planning
❏ Obtain intelligence of the area through various sources.
❏ Check with the embassy of the flag the ship flies for information

on local corruption. As a backup, check an online corruption index to get a reading on the general situation.

❏ Lay out your track and file from port of departure to port of destination.

❏ Link up with other vessels during transit through dangerous waters.

MARINER'S CHEAT SHEET OF
ANTIPIRACY PROCEDURES

❏ Call for assistance at the first signs of trouble. Know the frequencies (and preset them) of naval and coast guard forces in your area of operations (AO).

❏ Maintain a locked-down ship.

❏ Activate ShipLoc or Inmarsat security alert and tracking system; AIS (Automatic Identification System) should be on already.

❏ Set crew to antipiracy stations.

❏ Have antiboarding systems (e.g., LORAD, high-pressure hoses) ready.

❏ Have nonlethal and lethal weapons on station.

❏ Maneuver out of the danger area at the highest safe speed.

❏ Fishtail the boat to make boarding more difficult and create a wake that will cause problems for smaller craft following.

❏ Fire red distress flares, initiate Grimes lights and strobes, and set off the ship's horn so that other craft in the area know you are in distress.

❏ Illuminate your craft to attract attention to it.

❏ Use nonlethal deterrents to repel pirate boats trying to come alongside to board. Fire flare guns at pirates. Try to foul props of pirate skiffs with flotsam. Use high-pressure hoses.

❏ Return fire if weapons are used against you and if you have weapons available.

❏ Use the most frequently used routes with a large amount of traffic and sail through those areas when traffic is heaviest.

❑ Convoy with other vessels if possible.
❑ If pirates begin to board, shut down engines and retreat crew to safe room.

It is essential for the master who will be sailing into dangerous waters to establish a liaison with naval forces operating in the AO. For example, MV ships entering the Gulf Aden and Indian Ocean usually register four to five days before transit with the following organizations:

UK Maritime Trade Operations (UKMTO)
http://www.rncom.mod.uk/Maritime_Operations/UK_Trade_Opera-tions.aspx
e-mail: ukmtodubai@eim.ae
Tel: +971 50 552 3215 or +971 50 552 6007
Fax: +971 4 306 5710

UKMTO is the first point of contact for ships in the AO for day-to-day interface between masters and naval forces.

Maritime Security Centre—Horn of Africa (MSCHOA)
http:// www.mschoa.org
e-mail: postmaster@mschola.org
Tel: +44 (0) 1923 958545
Fax: +44(0) 1923 958520

MSCHOA is the operation center for European Union naval forces monitoring commercial shipping traffic through the Gulf of Aden.

Maritime Liaison Office (MARLO)

http://www.cusnc.navy.mil/marlo/
e-mail: marlo.bahrain@me.navy.mil
Tel: + 973 1785 3925
Fax: +973 1785 3930

MARLO is out of Bahrain and operates as a base for information exchange between combined maritime forces (CMF) and the commercial shipping industry in the region.